A HARROWSMITH GARDENER'S GUIDE

GROUND COVERS

EDITED BY JENNIFER BENNETT

ILLUSTRATIONS BY MARTA SCYTHES

CAMDEN HOUSE

Reprinted 1988

Canadian Cataloguing in Publication Data

Main entry under title:

Ground Covers

(Harrowsmith gardener's guides)
Includes index
ISBN 0-920656-68-4

1. Ground cover plants. 2. Lawns. I. Bennett,
Jennifer. II. Series.

SB432.G76 1987   635.9'64   C87-093548-8

Trade distribution by
Firefly Books
3520 Pharmacy Avenue, Unit 1-C
Scarborough, Ontario
Canada M1W 2T8

Printed in Canada for
Camden House Publishing
(a division of Telemedia Publishing Inc.)
7 Queen Victoria Road
Camden East, Ontario
K0K 1J0

Design by
Linda J. Menyes

Cover by
Jonathan Milne

Colour separations by
Herzig Somerville Limited
Toronto, Ontario

Printed and bound in Canada by
D.W. Friesen & Sons
Altona, Manitoba

Acknowledgements

The Harrowsmith Gardener's Guide to Ground Covers is a cooperative effort that could not have been completed without the dedicated work of many people. They include art director Linda Menyes; artist Marta Scythes, who prepared the botanical sketches; assistant editor David Archibald; typesetter Patricia Denard-Hinch; graphic artist Susan Gilmour; copy editors and associates Sara Perks, Charlotte DuChene, Mary Patton, Cathy De Lury, Sharon McFadzean, Betty Robinson, Katharine Ferguson, Peggy Denard; executive editor Frank Edwards; assistant editor Denise Fisher; publisher James Lawrence; and Adèle Crowder, curator of the Queen's University Herbarium.

Contents

Chapter One:
Thinking Low

By Helen Molitor

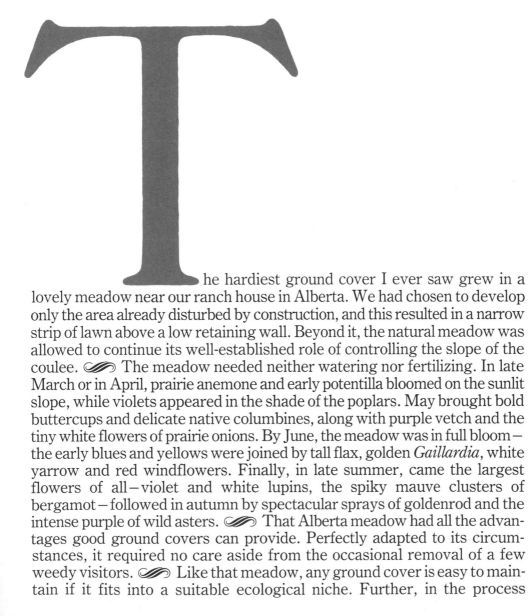

he hardiest ground cover I ever saw grew in a lovely meadow near our ranch house in Alberta. We had chosen to develop only the area already disturbed by construction, and this resulted in a narrow strip of lawn above a low retaining wall. Beyond it, the natural meadow was allowed to continue its well-established role of controlling the slope of the coulee. ✑ The meadow needed neither watering nor fertilizing. In late March or in April, prairie anemone and early potentilla bloomed on the sunlit slope, while violets appeared in the shade of the poplars. May brought bold buttercups and delicate native columbines, along with purple vetch and the tiny white flowers of prairie onions. By June, the meadow was in full bloom — the early blues and yellows were joined by tall flax, golden *Gaillardia*, white yarrow and red windflowers. Finally, in late summer, came the largest flowers of all — violet and white lupins, the spiky mauve clusters of bergamot — followed in autumn by spectacular sprays of goldenrod and the intense purple of wild asters. ✑ That Alberta meadow had all the advantages good ground covers can provide. Perfectly adapted to its circumstances, it required no care aside from the occasional removal of a few weedy visitors. ✑ Like that meadow, any ground cover is easy to maintain if it fits into a suitable ecological niche. Further, in the process 7 of fitting into such specialized environments, ground covers solve all sorts of landscape problems involving soil, sun and temperature. They can do so because they exist everywhere in nature. The undercanopy of the forest floor, the prairie meadow and the dune grasses of beaches are all ground covers, as are the most highly managed fairways and greens of modern golf courses. Any low-growing vegetation that

*Deciduous and evergreen shrubs as well as scores of herbaceous plants, such as hen and chickens (*Sempervivum spp)*, lend colour and texture to the landscape.*

prevents soil and water loss by blanketing an area is a ground cover: lawns, vines and matting creepers, dwarf shrubs, mounding ornamental grasses, wild and domesticated perennials, self-seeding annuals and even herbs and other ground-hugging edibles. The only requirement is that the vegetation be low-growing (usually less than 18 inches tall), since taller plants tend to have woody stems which raise the foliage well above ground level, allowing the growth of other plants beneath. Also, the best ground cover plants have some means of spreading, such as by overground rooting stems, like thymes; by runners, like strawberries; by underground stems known as rhizomes, like irises; or by moving outward in a clumping fashion.

Many grasses are both low-growing and spreading, and despite the variety of ground covers that exists, lawns remain by far the most popular, blanketing perhaps 100,000 square miles in North America alone. In part, this is a matter of habit and prestige, but it is also because grass – usually a mixture of different grasses – is the most durable vegetation under the stress of foot traffic. In fact, on the racecourses of Europe, grass is the only vegetation that can endure the onslaught of tons of horseflesh thundering along to the finish line, race after race, sometimes for days on end.

Another advantage of lawns, one usually ignored in gardening books, is that they are safe. The lawns of good nursing homes are testimony to this: dotted with wooden or wicker furniture and with colourful displays of annuals, they allow even people in wheelchairs easy access to the outdoors. Lawns are safe for infants too. Some years ago, two young friends of mine, rejecting their parents' suburban way of life, vowed never to grow anything as orderly as a lawn. This resolve lasted until their first child started to crawl. The baby's shrieks as she encountered yet another emergent thistle or sharp-edged stone persuaded her parents that perhaps a small patch of sod would constitute an acceptable compromise.

Despite their advantages, grasses do require a great deal of maintenance. And lawns can be overdone, even boring. Fortunately, there are many other sorts of ground covers in many sizes, colours and textures. They lack grasses' durability underfoot. Creeping thyme and chamomile are often called as tough as grass, but, in my experience, they will not stand up to such exuberances as the impromptu games of touch football or soccer that I've seen in every neighbourhood I have lived in. Yet vines and low shrubs, herbs and wildflowers offer other sorts of hardiness as well as beauty, versatility and charm.

In dry areas prone to drought, artemisias, thymes and junipers thrive, while, as

*Among the wildflowers in textured garden "scenes" are violets (*viola spp).

many gardeners know, the very best place to plant mint is right under an outside faucet, in that soggy patch where nothing else will grow. Dune grasses, heathers, the popular bugleweed, chamomile, even certain ivies and the incredibly tough creeping roses all survive both sand and salt. To me, nothing is more surprising than finding, just in the lee of storm-swept dunes, the hardy relatives of such pampered darlings as the hybrid tea roses.

Woodland ground cover plants, creatures of partial shade and acidic soil, are numerous since the woodland habitat is one of the largest in the world. Perhaps the favourite is the periwinkle (*Vinca minor*), used especially under trees where mowing is awkward. But the woodland plants I find most impressive are the common and variegated pachysandras and the attractive, if unpleasantly named, goutweed, which will grow even under the notoriously unneighbourly maples.

In addition to solving various dilemmas of soil, shade and temperature, ground covers allow the gardener to cope with all sorts of landscaping problems. For example, my Alberta wildflowers prevented soil erosion, as did a series of small terraced plantings of heather, whose sturdy roots were impervious even to the rivulets that ran directly over and among them for part of every day in spring.

Such cover plantings can conceal or transform harsh angles and other unattractive features created by commercial land use, as The Butchart Gardens near Victoria, British Columbia, dramatically demonstrates. There, on the side of what was once a commercial limestone quarry, a superb sunken garden fills much of the original pit. Edgar Dash, one of the gardens' horticulturists, considers the wide range of ground covers an essential part of the gardens' success. He lists among his favourites "the vincas, naturally. And we like ajugas, which are vigorous but easy to control because of their shallow roots, and the pachysandras, whose foliage is so attractive that one hardly notices the small flowers of some varieties. Bearberry, junipers and St. John's wort are also some of our standbys. And, of course, we are fortunate in being able to grow English ivy. In fact, as your readers probably know, it covers the ground here and then starts growing up walls and tree trunks if we don't watch it."

In the home garden, on a much smaller scale, ground covers will fill the nooks and crannies of a rocky slope and produce colour between the flagstones of a patio or pathway. Further, mixed plantings of ground covers not only provide a variety of different types of roots for better soil control but above ground create an appealing variety of textures and depths. In some Vancouver gardens there are textured "scenes" that take advantage of the variety of ground covers available. The most popular, often just behind a magical hedge, is a flagstoned or pebbled area surrounded by a woodland glade, like a setting for *A Midsummer Night's Dream*. There, violets, sweet woodruff or polyanthus primroses form the lowest layer, backed by larger-leaved plantings of hostas, wild ginger and trilliums. These groupings, in turn, give way to ferns or, in one spectacular example I remember, golden St. John's wort. Beyond, either tall bushes or walls enveloped in ivy complete the illusion, while the necessary shade is provided by four or five carefully selected trees.

Planning before planting ensures that lower plants grow in front of taller ones.

Designing

Such living works of art help to remind gardeners that establishing ground covers is not just a matter of throwing some seeds on the wayside. A ground cover planting is like any perennial planting: a badly planned one can be disastrous, while a well-planned one will last and delight for a lifetime.

If a mixed planting of ground covers is anticipated, the first stage is design, a subject that has raised more conflicts in paradise than anything since the apple. One easy way to design is to start small, perhaps with a single flowerbed or with a patch from which the sod has been stripped back. Any mistakes can then be corrected before a larger project is undertaken. If a small start is impossible, a visit to local parks or botanical gardens can suggest attractive combinations of locally hardy plants. So, too, a book on

landscape design will help, as may a brief summary of the basic principles of ground cover design. Here are some points to keep in mind:

•Place the lowest, smallest-leaved plants in front, moving back and up into taller, broader leaves and finally into low bushes and shrubs.

•Remember that massed plantings are generally more attractive than a single specimen or a busy scattering of small clumps. Masses are not only aesthetically pleasing but are also easier to maintain and more attractive to birds.

•Aim for interesting visual effects. Try to create a harmonious variety of colours, heights and shapes of leaves and a sense of pleasantly relaxed, free-form contours. The most boring planting I ever saw was a semicircle of heather rimmed with rigidly geometric plantings, first of thyme and then of thrift, both shaped into perfect mounds. Far more attractive is a flowing interplay of ground covers as in the Vancouver "forest glades."

•Consider the dimension of time as well as space. The right selection of evergreen and deciduous plants will provide spring flowers, summer berries, fall colour and winter cover.

In designing such forms, graph paper helps, but a three-dimensional model is even more useful. I have constructed several landscapes from papier-mâché, grass shavings, moss and miniature evergreen and deciduous trees bought from model-train shops. I lay out the papier-mâché as the ground, gluing down grass clippings to represent any lawn area I plan to retain; then, with moss and dismantled miniature trees, I try various loose arrangements of free forms until I have a useful model of what seems to be the most pleasing.

Planting

Before any planting begins on a new site, a soil test is a good investment. Provincial departments of agriculture and state extension services can tell you where to go, what to do, what will be charged and what results to expect. Usually, the test results tell the pH level of the soil—its acidity or alkalinity—and which nutrients are present or lacking. People do, of course, simply plunge ahead, inserting pockets of enriched soil in what seems to be a sandy, dry bank, or filling plastic liners with highly acidic, humus-rich soil for woodland natives. But such challenging of natural conditions immediately entails very high maintenance, and after all, one of the purposes of carefully chosen ground covers is to cut labour.

Ideally, organic soil preparation begins in the fall, when repeated tilling every two or three weeks exposes as many weed seeds as possible. In the spring, do a final tilling (or turning with a spade) as soon as the soil has thawed, and dig in an inch-deep dressing of compost or manure, add-ing a light dusting of bone meal for good root development if the soil is low in phosphate. Healthy plants, rather than those urged into hothouse hyperactivity by overfertilization, should be the aim.

Evergreens and woody shrubs are usually planted in early spring before the buds have opened, although evergreens can also be planted after leaf drop in fall. For other ground covers, the traditional times of mid- to late May—or as soon as the soil is dry enough to work and heavy frosts have passed—are appropriate.

In my experience, staggered rows of plants always cover ground more efficiently and beautifully than do straight rows. The spacing will vary considerably, from less than a foot between the smallest plants to 3 feet between shrubs such as cotoneaster, juniper and euonymus and 5 feet or more between tall, vigorous vines. The space between the centre of one plant and its closest neighbour should allow each *mature* plant to overlap some 5 to 10 percent with the next. In the early years, low-growing annuals may fill the spaces between perennials. Sometimes, interesting effects can be obtained by deliberately underspacing a little; slightly crowded junipers, for example, tend to mound rather than sprawl, but they also require supplementary fertilizer to remain healthy.

As soon as they are planted, all perennials require extra water to ensure healthy rooting. The watering should be deep, so that the soil is wet at least 2 or 3 inches below the lowest root level. Apply drip irrigation or a fine spray for several hours. Shrubs, of course, can be heavily watered by bucket, to help eliminate any air pockets left after planting. After this initial watering, water deeply once a week until the plants are established and growing, and thereafter only as required for the species—some thrive on dry soil.

On slopes, where even careful watering might cause erosion of newly planted ground, spread strips of jute over the plantings until they take hold. Rolls of jute 11

Occasional weeding, annual clipping and the addition of compost in spring will keep wildflower meadows lush and colourful.

wintercreeper and moss pink, benefit from an annual mowing, but since the plants should be cut no shorter than 6 inches, a nylon line trimmer is the most useful tool for the job (for small areas, hedge clippers serve). A few plants such as Oregon grape benefit from an early spring pruning, and ungainly vines of clematis or ivy can also be trimmed then. After a heavy rain, older artemisias may break open and sprawl limply; cutting them back by 3 to 6 inches will encourage new, compact growth.

Other maintenance might include an application of compost each spring if the planting seems to require it. A light grass rake is most useful for this and can also be used to thin out trash or thatch or to spread a mulch between the plants until they have matured and blanketed the area. Mulches such as pebbles, shredded bark and wood chips are attractive as well as useful. In regions where winter freezes and thaws alternate, it may be advisable to apply a winter mulch once the ground is frozen; the usual protection consists of evergreen branches or straw.

Propagation

Division is a simple process that can be used with many ground covers, plants whose natural tendencies to spread can be exploited by the gardener. To divide a plant, either dig it up and pull it apart, or simply push the point of a trowel into a natural division in the plant and remove part of it, planting the removed part elsewhere. In the case of ajugas and similar plants that grow outward from the centre and eventually turn brown in the middle, divisions taken from the edge can replace the fading core. Clumping ground covers like hostas need to be lifted and divided every three to five years so that they do not become too crowded and starved for soil nutrients.

Some ground covers can be fairly easily propagated by cuttings. Usually this is a

can be purchased (or occasionally rented) from local nurseries and are easily fastened in place with wire coat hangers cut in half, the lower bar bent back and plunged into the earth. The hook of the hanger enables the gardener to remove it easily when its task is completed.

Thereafter, maintenance is usually limited to weeding around the plants until they become well enough established to crowd out invaders on their own. An occasional pruning of most species will make the plants bushier, more dense and better ground covers. A few plants, like

*Perhaps the favourite cover for partial shade and acidic soil is the periwinkle (*Vinca minor*), which is especially suitable under trees where mowing is awkward.*

fairly slow process, although some plants such as *Vinca minor* and some sedums seem so eager to take root that bits of stem inserted into damp soil in the garden quickly establish themselves and spread. In other cases, take a 4-inch stem tip that includes at least one leaf node, wet the base and dip it in rooting hormone powder (available in garden stores), and plant it in a pot of wet growing medium. Enclose the pot in a plastic bag, and place it in shade until cutting growth begins. Tug gently on the cuttings to determine whether they have begun to root, and when they have, remove the bag. Keep the rooted cuttings watered on a bright, warm window ledge until growth is well under way. The rooted cuttings should then be gradually introduced into their outdoor environment before they are planted permanently.

A few ground covers are quite easily grown from seed, either quickly, like annual alyssums, or slowly, like hostas. Alyssum can be sown directly where it will grow, but the perennial ground covers are best sown indoors, in damp potting soil, and kept in a bright place until the seedlings are large enough to be transplanted outdoors. As a general rule, bury the seeds twice the depth of their diam-

eter; tiny seeds such as thymes can be broadcast on the soil surface and lightly misted until they germinate. Some ground covers self-sow, providing more of their kind in perpetuity and requiring only that the gardener remove seedlings where they are not wanted.

Using ground covers other than lawns, then, need not be overly expensive, provided one has the patience and the desire to multiply plants at home. Economy can be added to the list of other ground cover qualities, which includes versatility, tenacity and usefulness in otherwise difficult landscape situations. But I think the greatest attribute of ground covers is their beauty. My wildflower meadow was a constant source of delight, not only when in bloom during the warm months but even in winter when it provided shelter and food for birds and for small animals of many sorts. If lawns meet our need for order and constancy, then even the most modest planting of other ground covers helps fulfill our desire for variety and change.

Helen Molitor grows her garden in Winnipeg and teaches English at the University of Manitoba.　13

Chapter Two:
Please Step on the Grass

By Ken McMullen

y favourite lawn is the cool green sward of the Alberta legislature in Edmonton. On a summer's day, I saw it surrounded by dry prairie and scattered with joggers, strollers and friends kept in synchrony by a carillon that rang the time from the building's tower. An irrigation system, fed from the North Saskatchewan River, pumped tons of water onto the grass all day long. Stepping onto this soothing lawn from the native prairie grasses – wild plants that were dormant or had gone to seed and dried to a bright yellow – vividly demonstrated the difference between wild grasses and the domestic ones that stay green (if watered) throughout the summer and well into winter. ∽ Almost every home has a little piece of such grassy luxury, watered and fertilized to oasis hue. I presume many of these lawns are grown because their owners like them; perhaps some people even enjoy mowing and watering. There are many others, though, who find the maintenance of such perfection a summer-long burden but do not realize that their lawns need not be as immaculate as those around public buildings, that the occasional weed can be quite beautiful and that a small lawn, properly positioned and of the right size, can be as useful as – and considerably less work than – a large one. After all, how many homeowners actually jog in their backyards? ∽ The idea of growing 15

While providing a soothing complement to vertical elements in the garden's landscape, grass blends in well with other low-growing plants both in shade and in full sun.

one's own grassy meadow was imported from damp, cool western Europe, where early lawns had a very practical purpose. Distrustful nobles cleared away the forest from around their houses so they could see who was coming to visit. The land, stripped of mature trees, reverted to grassland. The grass was then scythed short in case someone came visiting, perhaps crawling on his belly holding a longbow and arrow. The cut grass created pleasing green expanses surrounding the stately homes and castles. Cricket, tennis, croquet and lawn bowling became the recreational activities of those with enough grassy expanse to accommodate a rolling ball and several players. During the Industrial Revolution, the emerging landed middle class adopted the broad green lawn, even though its purpose was, by then, obscure. If a man's home was his castle, it simply had to be surrounded by grass. In North America today, this is still true. A good lawn is an important social statement—in fact, the chemical lawn-care industry has grown by about 25 per-

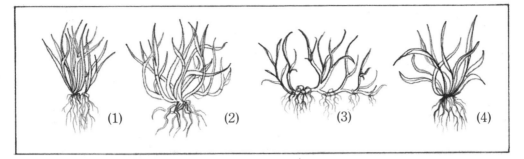

Most lawns are mixtures of different grasses. Fescues (1) spread slowly into tufts; bent grasses (2) grow outward and then up; creeping grasses like Kentucky bluegrass (3) spread by rhizomes to form strong turf; and rye grass (4) is fast-growing but short-lived.

cent each year for the last decade.

But it is no fault of grass if we think of it as something that must be doused with chemicals. I think of grass as a healer. I have noticed that a scar on the earth is quickly colonized by plants such as grasses. Compacted soil in heavy traffic areas is protected by low, sprawling grass. Grass fills cracks in concrete and holds riverbanks together. Cats and dogs eat grass when they are ill. Grasses can even heal themselves more rapidly than other plants, because their meristematic (growth) tissue is close to the ground, allowing them to be mowed without harm. Grasses are survivors. As the earth dries in summer, annual grasses produce seeds, while perennial species become dormant and dried. Both renew growth once the wet fall weather arrives. When the ground freezes, the plants "hibernate," waiting for the first thaw of spring. Plants that survive winter die-off, snow mould and fungi then grow quickly, spreading during the very damp early-spring-runoff time and quickly building rich, fertile topsoil for succession plants such as bushes and trees.

Despite their advantages, however, grasses are very modest plants. Many of us can identify a trillium or a fireweed, but few know even the most common wild grasses. They are simply there in the background, like rocks or stumps. Yet, when it comes to preparing a lawn, knowledge of grasses, the most durable of ground covers, is important.

Types of Lawn Grass

There are several species of grass used for lawns and many variations within those species, with yearly improvements bringing new cultivars that are more disease- and weather-resistant and longer-standing. Grasses can be divided roughly into two types: those that spread by stolons (over-ground runners) or rhizomes (underground roots) and those that form bunches, their new shoots originating within the sheaths of already-existing stems. Spreading types, like bluegrass, will form a sod and will heal easily from injury, while clumping types stay nicely in place, an advantage in some situations. Most lawns are blends of various seeds so that the best qualities of several types can be combined and complete loss of the lawn from diseases, drought or insects will not occur.

•Kentucky bluegrass (*Poa pratensis*), the most important and widely used turf grass in Canada and the northern United States, is very winter-hardy and tolerates drought, high and low temperatures, disease and wear and tear. A Eurasian native introduced to Kentucky in the 19th century, it grows from spreading rhi- 17 zomes and is attractive and durable. Bluegrass has its weaknesses, though: it can take as long as 28 days to germinate, and it does not tolerate shade, wetness or extremes of acidity or alkalinity. Many cultivars of bluegrass are available, and a mix of two or three carefully selected types can produce an ideal lawn for almost any short-season area. For instance, cultivars of bluegrass with natural resistance to mould include 'Banff' (Pickseed), 'Cheri' (Maple Leaf Mills), 'Dormie' (Pickseed, Newfield), 'Sydsport' (Oseco) and 'Touchdown' (Pickseed); cultivars that are tolerant of drought include 'Dormie,' 'Emmundi' and 'Fylking' (the latter two from Maple Leaf Mills); those with some shade tolerance include 'Nugget' and 'Touchdown' (both from Pickseed); those that can take a beating include 'Banff,' 'Emmundi,' 'Fylking' and 'Sydsport'; and those tolerant of cold winters, 'Dormie' and 'Emmundi.' 'Fylking' is a cultivar that is especially tolerant of road salt.

•Creeping red fescue and Chewings fescue (*Festuca* spp) are widely used, too, as lawn grasses. These fescues will tolerate lower levels of maintenance, poorer soil and less grooming than will bluegrass. Fescues germinate quickly, are the most shade-tolerant of grasses, will survive drought, withstand heavy traffic and hold a dark green colour that blends well with the bluegrasses. Creeping red fescue is a spreading grass, but Chewings tends to clump. Both are usually mixed with other species like bluegrass.

•Clover (*Trifolium repens*) is not a grass but a legume, a plant capable of supplying its own nitrogen. Grasses require that nitrogen be added to the soil. A lawn of clover and perennial grasses does not look as smooth and uniform as an all-grass lawn, but it requires no fertilizer, little water and less maintenance than an all-grass one. Clover withstands mowing well and remains green even during severe droughts. In her book *Green Thoughts* (Vintage Books, New York, 1981), El-

The large lawn surrounding the Alberta Legislature is immaculate but demanding.

eanor Perényi speaks most highly of clover as a lawn plant: "I discovered the virtues of clover by accident, when it began to appear in the lawn some years ago. Soon, the green tide had spread, and now I do all I can to encourage it, even to braving the high cost of the seed."

•Perennial rye grass (*Lolium perenne*) germinates extremely quickly (in as few as five days) and rapidly stabilizes newly seeded lawns, so it is sometimes mixed with other grasses as a nurse crop. So wear-tolerant that it is used for sports fields, it is not as winter-hardy as bluegrass and forms clumps rather than spreading by stolons or rhizomes. It may die out after about five years. Recently introduced varieties are fine-leaved, dark green and more winter-hardy.

•Annual rye grass germinates in 5 to 10 days and is generally used only as a starter; like other annuals, it lives only a year and so will leave gaps in the turf the following spring, allowing the perennial grasses to take over. A small percentage of annual rye grass included in a mixture for new lawns quickly stabilizes the area and gives an initial green cover.

• Bent grass (*Agrostis* spp) requires cool, moist conditions and so is grown only in places where summer temperatures are generally lower than 85 degrees F, such as England and the Pacific Northwest, or where it can be given a great deal of care, such as on golf greens, where it tolerates mowing to ¼ inch. Susceptible to snow mould and thatching, since it spreads by stolons, it requires a great deal of watering, fertilizing and dethatching and should be avoided for most home situations.

• Other lawn grasses include Russian wildgrass and streambank wheatgrass, dryland species used in the Brown and Dark Brown soil zones of the prairies, where soil moisture is very limited and watering may not be possible. Sheep's fescue (*Festuca ovina vulgaris*), another possible lawn species, is a blue-green, narrow-leaved, very coarse, drought-resistant grass that can be used on impoverished, dry, rocky sites where watering is impractical. Redtop grass (*Agrostis alba*) forms a coarse open sod and spreads by rhizomes. It is well suited to acidic soils and poorly drained areas, and it grows rapidly after seeding.

Within three or four years, a selection of easy-care grasses of the genera *Poa* and *Festuca* will become available. These grasses, selected by Jan Weijer, a geneticist at the University of Alberta, grow quickly to only a few inches tall and then slow down, requiring little mowing. They also have low requirements for watering and feeding, resist weeds and withstand traffic well.

Making a Lawn

Lawns differ from stands of wild grasses in three ways, as described by the editors of *Organic Gardening* magazine in *Lawn Beauty the Organic Way* (Rodale, 1970): first, lawns are a cultivated crop; second, they owe their quality to vegetative rather than sexual reproduction; and third, they must stay put, while grasses in nature can migrate. These factors mean that in planning, execution and care, a lawn must be treated like any other crop or like a vegetable or flower garden.

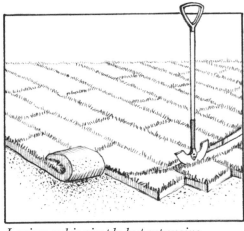

Laying sod is simple but expensive.

You must first decide where you wish to grow grass, how large you want the lawn to be and where the foot traffic will be heaviest – or where you would like it to be directed – ideal places for paths or other paving. Even grass will become thin or die out entirely if it is constantly underfoot. Flower borders, trees, vegetable and herb gardens will also, of course, reduce the amount of space that will be planted in lawn. Other ground covers described throughout this book may be attractive, require less maintenance and be well suited to difficult-to-mow or shady areas under hedges, along fences, under mature trees and next to the house. Consider your needs for a lawn carefully, and consider the limitations of your property and climate.

Turf grass does not grow well in shade, where it becomes thin and yellowish, with open patches of ground eventually showing through. Invasion by shade-tolerant 19

In preparing to plant a healthy and aesthetically pleasing lawn, gardeners should consider their soil type and climatic conditions before selecting grass species.

volunteers, such as annual bluegrass and rough bluegrass, will show as distinct thick patches during the growing season, and patches injured by snow mould in spring. Susceptible to diseases, such as leaf spot on red fescue or powdery mildew on Kentucky bluegrass, shaded turf also has a poor root system, so it is easily ripped out by foot traffic or leaf raking. Accept the fact that you will not have a first-class lawn in heavy shade. Pruning lower tree limbs and removing upper tree limbs can increase sunlight on the ground.
•Consider, too, how dry your climate is, how much watering you are willing to do and whether the watering of lawns is restricted in your area in summer. Perhaps you will opt for a larger patio and a smaller lawn, maybe even build a pond that can be used as a water reservoir. My backyard includes a fishpond whose water, with its nitrogen-rich droppings, can be poured on the lawn. Where you do

want lawn, a combination of Russian wild rye grass and red fescue may not look as neat as Kentucky bluegrass in spring but will survive summer in better condition.
•If the ground where the lawn will go is covered by weeds or trash, it should first be cleared. This may mean lifting sections of weedy ground with a shovel or pitchfork, shaking the soil loose and discarding the weeds; or it may mean covering the entire area in black plastic, which will kill all the plants under it in a season, leaving a dead thatch. Till and improve the soil before sodding or seeding. It is also possible to scratch seed into an existing lawn to augment the turf: for a small lawn, one need only drag a sharp-tined rake over the surface, while a larger area should be treated by a scarifying machine, also called a turf thinner or vertical mower, which can be rented from some garden-supply shops. Set the machine to scratch ¼ inch into the soil surface; then seed at

from becoming established and, when it is turned under the following spring, makes the soil more fertile and friable.

If the topsoil has been entirely removed from your property, spread purchased topsoil evenly over the subgrade to a depth of 6 inches. A simple drag ladder, built from two 6-foot lengths of 2 by 4 and weighted with a large stone, can be used to grade and firm the soil. Drag the ladder sideways across the area in both directions and on the diagonal to move the soil from high spots into the depressions and provide a firm, even soil base.

The most suitable time to seed lawns in most northern areas is from mid-August to mid-September, "the real beginning of the growth cycle" for turf, says the past president of the Lawn Institute, Dr. Robert W. Schery. Early spring is also satisfactory. Spring and early June are recommended for the prairies and mid-west; early fall and early spring for the Pacific coastal areas. Sow the seed at the rate recommended on the package. For a small area, simply scatter the seed by hand as evenly as possible. For a large area, rent a drop seeder and sow half the seeds in one direction and the rest at right angles to the first. Cover the seeds lightly, and roll the seedbed with an empty lawn roller. Mulch with a light layer of straw, pine boughs or chopped twigs – materials that will stall the soil's erosion and drying while the seeds germinate.

the rate for a new lawn, fertilize and soak the area thoroughly.

•Loam soil, preferably about 6 inches deep, provides the best bed for a new lawn, ensuring ample water percolation, drainage of excess moisture, sufficient oxygen for growth and good texture for rooting. Loam is amply supplied with soil microorganisms that are important in the breakdown of grass clippings. Clay soil develops wet areas and puddles, while sandy soil makes drought conditions worse and may require extra fertilization. Both types of soil can be improved with compost and other organic matter. It may also be necessary to purchase topsoil, but there is a less expensive method that can be employed by patient lawn makers. Before I sow grass seed, I prefer to build the soil by first planting a green-manure crop, such as annual rye grass or clover, in the early fall; this protects the surface of the soil from erosion, prevents the weeds

Until the seedlings become well established, keep the seedbed damp but not saturated. Mow for the first time when the seedlings are about 3 inches tall. Take care with the first mowing, as the plants will still be very tender. The soil should be dry and firm to avoid damage to the seedlings from your feet and the mower. From then on, set the mower to cut at 2 or 3 inches, a good height to keep the lawn attractive and reasonably drought-proof.

Sod is more expensive than seed and is not usually grown to organic standards for commercial sale; however, it is instant, 21 easy to install at any time during the growing season, and it can be maintained organically once in place. Lay the first row along a straight line (such as a string, driveway or house), and offset the second row by half a sod, as if you were laying bricks. Lay the second row close to the first, just touching, not crowding; cut the sod with a hatchet or knife to fit odd places. Use stakes to hold sods to steep slopes. Flatten with a partially filled lawn roller to ensure that the roots are in contact with the soil, or for a small area, tramp over the sods. As Gervase Markham wrote in *A Way to Get Wealth* in 1613, the new sods should be "danced upon with the feete [so that] within a short time after, the grasse may begin to pepe

Flawless grass may be too demanding of nature, which favours diversity and change.

up and put foorth small haires . . . . " Then water thoroughly. Do not let the sod dry out until the roots are well established, at which time the "small haires" will begin to grow rapidly.

From then on, the organic lawn-care routine begins in early spring, when you should rake the grass vigorously to clear away most debris. Too many tree leaves can smother grass. Remove the leaves and compost them, but don't bother raking after normal mowings, because the

clippings, a valuable source of nitrogen and other nutrients you have probably been applying to the lawn, will return fertility to the soil. If the clippings are so long that they leave clumps of "hay," however, do rake them and pile them to compost.

Fertilizers

Although lawns (if not pocketbooks) are said by government manuals to benefit from as many as five applications of fertilizer a year, many gardeners feed the grass only when it looks pale and have perfectly acceptable – if not lordly – lawns as a result. Studies by the Smithsonian Institution showed that a lawn given no care at all except regular 3-inch mowing was quite acceptable in appearance. One annual feeding, at most two, is enough for almost any lawn, although a lawn containing about half clover will need no fertilizer at all. If you do fertilize, note that the basic elements which should be applied are nitrogen, phosphorus and potassium; additional micronutrients abound in such fertilizers as compost, sludge and manure.

In general, organic fertilizers are superior to chemical ones because the organic nutrients are made available to plants through gradual breakdown by the soil microorganisms. They do not produce the immediate plant response that chemical fertilizers do, but nutrient uptake occurs over a longer time, eliminating feast-and-famine stress on the plants and encouraging the growth of healthy soil microorganisms. Compost, sludge and manure are, in fact, general-purpose soil builders that can be raked over the lawn at most twice a year, in a layer about ½ inch thick. •Nitrogen (N) is the element that produces a thick green lawn because it promotes the growth of leaf tissue and improves the general health of the plant. The equivalent of two pounds of nitrogen to 1,000 square feet of lawn is the most that should be required annually. The nitrogen level is especially high in organic

A well-maintained lawn offers recreational as well as landscaping possibilities.

below 6, most common in the east and wherever rainfall is heavy but less likely in drier areas. Add lime only if soil analysis indicates that the pH level needs to be raised to 6 or 6.5, the best level for lawn grasses and, indeed, for most plants. Use ground dolomitic (containing magnesium and calcium) or calcitic (with only calcium) limestone.

Mature bluegrass lawns may be fed in late April, mid-June and early September, when an ideal grass "dinner" contains two parts nitrogen to one part phosphorus and one part potassium. A "bedtime" feeding, in late October or early November, with a high-nitrogen fertilizer prepares the grass for winter and improves early-spring emergence. In shady areas, reduce by half the amount of nitrogen, and increase the amount of potassium to encourage root development and leaf growth. Fertilize trees and shrubs separately by making deep fertilizer holes.

Weeds

The fact that weeds are largely in the eye of the beholder is no comfort to most lawn owners who despair at patches of dandelions and creeping Charlie in their cherished front yard. Consider, though, that chemical pesticides are all dangerous – that is why they have so many warnings on the label – and that your desire for flawless grass may be a little too demanding of nature, which favours diversity and change. With that in mind, there are still ways to keep the lawn acceptably weedfree.

Because a thick lawn will smother most competitors, proper feeding and maintenance are the best organic weed-prevention measures. Build strong, healthy grass and soil, and bring out the trowel or dandelion cutter as soon as weeds are evident, rather than after they have established a stronghold. Watering infrequently or not at all in early spring and only to avoid drought stress in summer

fertilizers like blood meal, fish meal, manure, sludges such as Milorganite and seed meal such as linseed, soybean, cottonseed and peanut. Raw manure or concentrated manures (such as chicken) can burn grass by releasing nitrogen too quickly; compost these with high-cellulose materials such as straw or sawdust.

•Phosphorus (P) promotes general growth, especially of roots. Organic fertilizers that supply good amounts of phosphorus include ground rock phosphate (combine with manure for improved efficiency), colloidal phosphate, blood meal and bone meal.

•Potassium (K) aids plants' vigour and may improve grasses' winter hardiness and their tolerance of drought and disease. Potassium is found in greensand, granite dust, wood ashes, rock phosphate, kelp and plant residue, such as compost.

•Limestone is used to balance overly sour or acidic soil, which has a pH level 23 helps keep conditions amenable to grass and inhospitable to many other plants. If necessary, rearrange traffic patterns or build paths to reduce wear, which will produce empty spots ideal for weed invasion.

Dandelions, indicators of soil compaction and low surface-nutrient levels, may be the least loved of garden plants, despite their being bright and pretty in bloom. When the soil is very wet, pry out the entire plant or cut the taproot as far below the soil surface as possible. An old kitchen knife works well, and nurseries sell special tools for the purpose. (Hand weeding is another reason for keeping the lawn area fairly small.) Mow the flower stems frequently to stop them from seeding. Children can be usefully occupied gathering dandelions for pennies a dozen. If all else fails, remember that young dandelion greens are tasty steamed or in a salad and that the flowers make a very pleasant wine.

Pests

Some of the new grass cultivars are resistant to pests. There are perennial rye grasses and tall fescues, for instance, that are not damaged by sod webworms, billbugs, chinch bugs or by southern armyworms; however, white grubs, the larval stage of scarab beetles, can harm all types of grasses. Three varieties of scarabs are common in lawns in Canada and the northern United States: June beetles, European chafers and Japanese beetles. All emerge from late May to mid-June. June beetles have a three-year cycle and generally feed ravenously during the summer of their second year. European chafers feed in early spring and from late September until freeze-up. Japanese beetles damage roots in the spring and fall, when there is plenty of surface moisture. As the roots are destroyed by the grubs, sections of lawn wilt and turn brown and can easily be pulled back to reveal the grub beneath. Skunks and other small animals are the main or-

When the lawn's soil is quite wet, pry out dandelions or sever their roots deeply.

ganic control of white grubs. The animals do most of their hunting at night and leave behind little chunks of ripped-out sod that look as if they have held golf tournaments and did not replace their divots. Just retrieve the turf, pack it down and water.

Moulds, mildew and fungi are symptoms of a lack of air circulation, so increasing air movement over the turf is the surest control. This may involve thinning bushes and shrubs around mould-susceptible areas. Of course, air movement cannot be increased under snow, so snow mould is the most troublesome disease of northern lawns. Caused by several different low-temperature fungi – the snow mould on prairie lawns differs from that in the east – it is most conspicuous in spring when the snow is melting. Lawn areas become covered with a cottony growth, and in severe cases the grass is killed. When the areas are first visible after the snow melts, rake or brush the

According to one's preference, lawn grasses can be mowed to a short or medium height (best for shaded lawns), or allowed to reach their full height and go to seed.

infected, matted grass to improve aeration and aid recovery. Mowing and raking the lawn in late fall will help make it resistant to snow-mould damage.

In humid weather, powdery mildew fungi invade grass in the shade and in other areas of poor air circulation. At first, the upper sides of the leaves become coated with a grey-white cobweblike growth. Eventually, the leaves are covered, and a sizable area of the lawn appears white and later turns pale yellow. Powdery mildew is not fatal to the lawn and will disappear after mowing and with the return of less humid conditions. Pruning shade trees and improving air circulation will help prevent its recurrence. Also, there are grass cultivars resistant to all types of moulds.

Moss in a lawn generally indicates low fertility, too much shade or poor drainage. If you wish to get rid of it, rake it out and fill in the depression with topsoil, then fertilize and seed. Moss is, however, green and carefree, and the most conservation-oriented gardeners now leave it be, appreciating it as a fine ground cover.

There is no moss, of course, in the lawns of the Alberta legislative buildings. The prairies are not moss country, and in any case, such an invader would be spurned on this pristine expanse that, like all immaculate, chemical-treated lawns, supposedly mirrors the weedfree personalities of the people in the buildings it surrounds. My own lawns – two small patches of turf between vegetable gardens and areas of euonymus, spurge, ferns and wild ginger – reflect a more eclectic spirit. Like my life, my grass is unpredictable and imperfect, but like all grass, it is a healer of the soil and of my spirits.

Ken McMullen, the past-president of Canadian Organic Growers, cultivates his own lawns in Toronto, Ontario.

Chapter Three:
Wildflower Meadows

By Eva Hoepfner

eed catalogues tantalize with glossy photographs of massed wildflowers: brilliant combinations of red, blue, yellow, orange and purple, like samples of old-fashioned cotton prints. At the garden centre, shelves are stocked with cans, canvas bags, plastic sacks, even greeting cards of wildflower seeds. The containers are so appealing that their contents hardly matter. Articles in popular magazines rumour low maintenance, no fertilizer or water costs, ecological health and the attraction of wildlife. Your head starts to spin with visions of a gardener's paradise: gorgeous flowers waving among wispy grasses; birds, bees and butterflies darting and singing or humming through azure skies to nectar-laden blossoms, while you sit back contentedly with a long cool drink, at one with a healthy, wonderful world. Can wildflower meadows be the answer to a gardener's dreams? ◁▷ Well, the photographs don't lie, and the rumours are based on fact, but the truth is that a single meadow will not provide all attractions. A native prairie meadow, for example, requires little maintenance — but only after four years of intensive weeding; native grasses and flowers may be in harmony with nature, but they never achieve a gaudy display. The common commercial wildflower seed mixtures, on the other hand, will provide a Technicolor explosion of flowers — enough to stop traffic on an eight-lane 27

Gardeners often seek to imitate the beauty and diversity of natural meadows.

freeway – but only if they are planted on soil treated repeatedly with herbicide, which is not known to lure wildlife. Furthermore, the colourful splash of the mainly exotic flowers usually lasts less than two years. Between these two extremes of wildflower meadows lie many variations.

The wildflower meadow has only recently become part of a well-tended home landscape. It remains relatively untested, given the diverse climate and soil conditions across the land, but what most frequently turns a meadow into a minefield of dissatisfaction stems from differences in definition and expectations. What is a wildflower to you can be a noxious weed to the weed inspector, and what is a wildflower to your seed company may be a grass to you. As for appearance, one person's cherub is another's gnome. A meadow might inspire you with nostalgia or conservational righteousness, but it can equally incite your tidy neighbour to organize a vigilante mower brigade. Many lawsuits on record attest to the fact. Even Rodale Press, publishers of *Organic Gardening* magazine, were taken to court for growing a wildflower meadow in front of their Pennsylvania offices, contravening a local lawn ordinance.

Not long ago, a developer near Toronto agreed to turn parts of a new housing development into wildflower meadows. The object was to reduce maintenance needs and to make the buildings blend in with the natural parkland that weaves throughout the development. The town was enthusiastic, as were a good number of local residents. A wildflower-and-grass seed mixture was planted, but the exotic grasses in the mix greatly outnumbered the sprinkling of common alien flowers such as clover and yellow trefoil. It was not what many residents expected.

The following year, a different wild-

This example is not meant to discourage but to point out that often too much is expected too soon, with too little research and labour. Before you attempt a wildflower meadow, know exactly what effect you want, exactly what the seed company is selling you and how the meadow might affect your neighbour and your weed inspector. Walk ever so slowly – don't run – for a can, or whatever, of seed. If you are uninformed, you might not get what you bargained for.

Floral Definitions

Gardeners have long squabbled over what wildflowers are. Purists insist they are native plants that grew before the arrival of the Europeans. Others include naturalized plants – those introduced from other parts of the world and that reproduce freely in their non-native habitat. Still others proclaim wildflowers are plants that look good in a wildflower setting, such as daffodils and wallflowers, or plants that behave in a "wild" manner, that is, ones that grow and spread without much pampering, such as periwinkles. Opinion these days favours the middle definition, which includes native and naturalized plants. Weeds, incidentally, are just wildflowers that grow where they're not wanted. Noxious weeds are plants that the authorities have determined threaten human health or agricultural facility. Some common ones are Queen Anne's lace (*Daucus carota*), chicory (*Cichorium intybus*) and even ox-eye-daisy (*Chrysanthemum leucanthemum*).

flower mix was seeded into the existing meadow. The new mix contained mainly exotic annuals, with some perennials thrown in. The first year, most people were pleased with the results: a profusion of familiar garden flowers such as Shasta daisies, baby's-breath, phlox and bachelor's buttons mixed with naturalized plants like toadflax and yarrow. Only a few people were heard to grumble, "You call these wildflowers?" The second season, ragweed, burdock, thistles and poison ivy made a strong show, and complaints were heard all the way to the parks board. Few annuals had reseeded, and the perennials that had taken root were in a life-and-death struggle with the strong invaders. Some residents decided to take things into their own hands, and their mowers roared into action. The fate of the project is still uncertain, but the landscape contractor who planted the meadow swears he will never plant another.

The definition of "meadow" is also blurry. Some define it as a grassland occurring in areas of high rainfall, in contrast to "prairie," which occurs in areas of low rainfall; others say a meadow is a grassy spot found in forested regions. For our purposes, a meadow is a mixture of grasses and flowers growing in a sunny, open area.

For successful meadow gardening, it is important to understand natural processes. Most natural meadows are temporary stages in the ecological parade of succession. A bare field, left to its own devices, is soon invaded by grasses and forbs (nonwoody, broad-leaved plants like dandelions and plantain). This is the meadow stage. Soon shrubs and other woody seedlings will enter, and over the

Trilliums thrive in the shelter of woodland situations in fairly moist acidic soil.

next 50 to 150 years, the field will reach its climax stage, the forest. If you want a meadow to remain a meadow, you must intervene by weeding or burning it.

Sometimes, depending on climate, soil, moisture conditions and such other factors as seed availability, the presence of grazing animals and the occurrence of fire, the meadow stage becomes the climax. In North America, these natural grasslands are found in the prairies (*prairie* is French for "meadow"). The indigenous flora forms a plant community, a stable collection of diverse species that has evolved over the ages to adapt to the particular soil and climate of the area. They depend on each other for survival, tall plants sheltering short ones from sun and wind, ground-hugging plants protecting the soil from erosion, and all

manner of organic litter enriching the soil. The community is a complex interaction of plants, insects and soil organisms and plays host to abundant wildlife.

A meadow that comes closest to simulating the natural plant community of your region will require the least amount of maintenance. If you are looking for carefree summer days, and you do not care much how your meadow looks, the simplest choice is to let the lawn grow. Be forewarned that for a long time, this kind of meadow will look like an abandoned field, which some folks might call unkempt. It will yield a good crop of weeds: dandelions, quack grass, burdock, thistles and teasel are common invaders. But, depending on how close you are to wildflower seed sources, you might also be pleasantly surprised.

Alice Hayek of Cobourg, Ontario, reduced her lawn mowing to a winding path and received her share of weeds. But since the property lies in a rural area, it took only two years for the lawn to naturalize, without her aid, to a small meadow of black-eyed Susans, sunflowers, goldenrod, milkweed, asters, pink fleabane, butter-and-eggs, wild strawberries and violets. If you are not as fortunate, you can introduce mature wildflower plants, but they will face fierce competition from the naturalized forbs and grasses. An annual mowing to about 6 inches with a string trimmer (or a rented sickle-bar mower for large areas) will help keep woody species in check.

But many of us don't plant a meadow to avoid work; for some, it is a conservational concern. As far back as 1847, a prairie settler wrote, "The prairie flowers have strangely enough disappeared from open grounds, under the croppings of cattle and the clippings of the scythe. Only a half-dozen sorts were seen in a ride of 30 miles, and these straggling at great distances." By that time, attempts had already been made to transplant wildflowers into the garden. "A few years will deprive us of

Planting a meadow of only native species, such as lupins on a New Brunswick field, *can satisfy both conservationists and lovers of low maintenance.*

these beautiful flowers in their wild state, and unless they are domesticated, the next generation will not know what they were." The recent midwest prairie restoration movement has since made great strides toward saving the prairie ecosystem from extinction.

Planting a meadow of only native species can satisfy both conservationists and lovers of low maintenance. The only problem is that it takes a lot of time and effort to keep the weeds at bay until the plant community is secure. Larry Lamb, an ecology technician at the University of Waterloo, Ontario, laboured for four years establishing pathways, preparing seedbeds, introducing plants and seeds, propagating rare species and weeding his backyard prairie garden. An annual spring burn has helped reduce weeds, and now that the native plants have knit into a tight little community, the burn is about all that remains of the work.

Lamb's low-maintenance mini-prairie looks nothing like an abandoned field. In winter, russet grasses and seed heads lace the snow; during the rest of the year, wave after wave of over 200 species mark the passing seasons. "During the growing season," Lamb says, "an average of two species start blooming every day." Short flowers, like purple pasqueflower, birdsfoot violets and shooting stars, emerge in spring, followed by taller golden Alexanders, purple bergamot and fiery butterfly weed. By midsummer, Turk's-cap lily and blazing star edge up to be topped by giant prairie dock and sunflowers. Goldfinches, meadowlarks, hummingbirds and butterflies flit through grasses that range from knee-high to 10 feet tall.

Lamb lives on the outer edge of what was formerly natural prairie. "However," he says, "you can grow prairie plants where there never was prairie. And if prairie plants are unsuited to the area, just plant those species native to the region – check your field guides – and fight the woody stuff. Natural grassland occurs anywhere you go."

Native Meadows

Prairie gardeners agree that you cannot re-create the feel of the sweeping prairie on less than an acre. You can, however, plant any sunny well-drained spot with native plants. In fact, it is advisable to start small – with a former perennial border, for example, or a corner of the lawn – and in-

Non-native ox-eye-daisies are considered noxious weeds in some areas.

crease the meadow once you find out what grows well. Meadows look especially pleasant set off by a solid background such as a wall, a fence or a shrubbery. For visual interest, take advantage of land contours, perhaps creating a slope and adding a few shrubs, rocks or a bench. Paths add shape, invite closer scrutiny and facilitate weeding.

Make sure the area gets at least five hours of sun a day; less than that will result in spindly growth and little bloom. The soil should be neutral or slightly alkaline.

It must be well drained and not too rich if you want blossoms instead of leaves and grasses. Add organic matter to hard clay soils. If you are replacing a lawn, remove and compost it (rented sod cutters are a great help). Don't plough it under unless you plan to smother the area with plastic or thick layers of newspaper for at least a year. Try to remove all vestiges of lawn grasses, for each little rhizome that stays in the soil can generate a large grassy patch that will be extremely difficult to remove once the area is seeded. In fall or spring, till the area to a depth of 4 inches or more.

Weeds are the prime enemies of meadows. Before you seed, cover the prepared area with black plastic for at least three months to induce weed germination and subsequent smothering. If you are a very patient gardener, fallow the soil for a growing season: rake shallowly, water to encourage weeds, then cultivate; repeat several times to encourage as many weeds as possible to germinate. Before seeding, rake, just barely scratching the soil surface to minimize other weed seeds rising to the surface.

Plants can be introduced by seed or as mature specimens. The cheapest way is to use all seed, but you will have to wait a couple of years at least for the perennials to start blooming. Mature plants will give structure to the meadow and achieve earlier bloom, but they are expensive. Combine a few plants with seeds for results that are both inexpensive and fast.

Gathering your own seed from the wild is possible but not encouraged. Unless you have the skill, knowledge and patience required for proper harvesting and treatment, there is a definite risk of depleting an already scarce supply of native plant sources.

Opinions vary on the best order of plant introduction. Some prairie gardeners avoid aggressive natives like asters and coreopsis for the first two years until the more exacting plants have been established, but others do the opposite. Illinois ecologist Robert Betz, who has restored more than 300 acres of prairie, believes that aggressive native plants must move in first to overcome foreign weeds. This creates a more hospitable prairie environment for the delicate plants, which can coexist with aggressive natives but not with foreign invaders like dandelion and burdock.

To guarantee hardiness, try to obtain plants and seed produced as close to your area as possible – and do not forget the grasses. "It is important to include grasses," says Lamb, "to compete with aggressive natives and to lend support to the taller forbs – and they act as a good background for setting off the flowers. Prairie grasses are not really sod-forming; there are openings for forbs to take hold." Grasses are also essential where soil erosion is a problem. Grass-to-forb ratio can be anywhere from 50:50 to 80:20.

Seed for effect, sowing tall plants together, for example, or broadcast the area randomly for more natural results. Mix the seed with sand, sawdust or vermiculite to show where you have seeded. Rake again very gently, and tamp down by foot or with a roller. A light mulch of weed-free straw or sawdust helps secure the seed from wind and rain. To ward off birds, lay twiggy branches or string black thread across the area. Water lightly until the seeds sprout, and wait patiently.

The first year, a native meadow can be discouraging. No matter how diligently you've weeded, some weeds will defy your efforts. And, while the weeds are flourishing, your seeded species will stubbornly resist fleshing out. This is because prairie plants first develop strong root systems (some 20 feet deep) for protection against a harsh climate. As well, nature staggers some seed germination over a period of years. Don't give up. The second year should see a lot of grasses and some flowers in bloom. If you continue to weed (know your weeds!), you will be amply rewarded by the fourth year.

Prairie grasslands undergo frequent burning, a process that kills off alien plants but leaves native ones intact. Burning also warms the soil for earlier growth (prairie plants are notoriously slow to emerge in spring), adds nutrients in the form of ash and removes thatch that could eventually choke out smaller plants. If you can arrange for a fire permit, burn every three or four years in early spring. Pick a windless day, and stand by with a snow 33 shovel in case things get too hot. Larry Lamb built firebreaks right into his meadow: 4-inch-deep gravel paths surround prairie islands, which he burns one at a time.

In most situations, of course, burning is dangerous, not to mention illegal. If you cannot burn, mow to 6 inches every spring with a string trimmer or scythe, and compost the clippings.

Exotic Meadows

Conservation is well and good, but the prevalence of exotic wildflower seeds shows there are other reasons for wanting a meadow. Depending on where you grew up, re-creating the meadow of your memories often wins out over regional conservation. Seedsman Bill Aimers confirms this. "A disproportionate number of my customers talk nostalgically about the meadows of England or Germany or Holland," he says. I believe it. I spent my childhood in rural Germany, and nothing turns me into a homesick jelly faster than a reproduction of Monet's poppy fields.

There is nothing wrong with indulging yourself in a passion for foreign flowers, but be aware, nostalgic gardeners, that a meadow from a commercial mix will rarely resemble one from your childhood. One popular seed mixture contains lots of corn poppies and cornflowers – the mainstays of my favourite meadow – but along with these is a crowd of unrelated species: yellow North American coreopsis, evening primroses and black-eyed Susans, orange Siberian wallflowers, purple loosestrife, pink Mediterranean dame's rocket, red North African flax and more. Missing are the wispy grasses that formed the background of my childhood meadow. The gaudy display on the seed packet is a far cry from what I remember as a harmonious haze of golden stalks and scarlet blossoms.

No seed mixture, of course, can satisfy everyone. Many people want spectacular

colour – all the time and quickly. Hence, most commercial mixes strive for a maximum variety of hues throughout the season and feature lots of annuals that will bloom the first year. The inclusion of flowers that tolerate various growing conditions is supposed to ensure that at least something will grow everywhere. Not all species are expected to flourish, and few will over any length of time. While some dwindle, others may take over, and this can create unforeseen problems.

The trouble with introducing alien species into a region is that you never know how they will react. They can succumb to the climate, or they can naturalize in a quiet, reserved manner, or they can take over the land. Many of our common weeds – dandelions, Queen Anne's lace, chicory – were introduced from Europe or Asia. Purple loosestrife (*Lythrum salicaria*), imported from Europe as an ornamental, is becoming a serious pest in various regions, yet it is included in many wildflower seed mixes. We should also heed the warnings from foreign gardeners. Those scarlet corn poppies, for example, are supposedly the bane of every European farmer. What if they love their new environment in the prairie wheat fields too?

Even if an introduced alien doesn't ravage the countryside, it might crowd out other desirable species within your own meadow. Often this means replanting your meadow from scratch, and having gone to all that trouble once, you might be reluctant to repeat the process.

Before buying seed, make sure the package lists the species by name. Check in a reliable reference book for potential troublemakers such as lawn grasses. These are sometimes used as filler but will quickly choke out many flowers. For hardiness and longevity, select a mix with a mainstay of locally native perennials, and remember that the strength of a meadow lies in diversity: the more species you try, the better your chance of success.

34

Lawn grasses left unmowed will soon display a collection of tall flowering weeds.

Start with a small area, a flowerbed, for example, and study the effect before seeding large areas.

Planting a commercial mix is very much like planting a native meadow. The secret is starting with a clean seedbed. Aimers says the best way to achieve all that glorious colour is by spraying the area two or three times with a nonselective herbicide like Roundup, which kills all green plants on contact. Wait at least a week, then seed at the recommended rate and water. You will still have to weed (remember, you have killed only the plants, not the seeds). Alternatively, cultivate repeatedly or apply black plastic for three months.

Mow the meadow in late summer or late winter to help disperse seeds and open the area to light. (Do not burn after early spring, or you will kill most of the plants.) Reseed patchy places every couple of years—every year for continuous annual bloom—and keep weeding. Some people start from scratch every three or four years.

Seed mixtures are a good introduction to meadow gardening. They can supply many species you might not have con-sidered; they let you become familiar with the attendant pleasures and problems. But do not be afraid to experiment. Lighten up a flower mix with noninvasive grasses; temper an all-native mixture with well-mannered naturalized flowers. Add a profusion of spring bulbs for early bloom. If you are cramped for space, forget the seeds, and create the essence of a meadow with a tidy little patch of perennial flowers and clumped grasses, each plant as carefully placed as in a perennial border.

There is one more thing. "Who," asked William Robinson in *The Wild Gardener* of 1894, "would not rather see the waving grass with countless flowers than a close surface without a blossom." Well, your neighbours might. Tell them of your plans, show them that you work hard (at least initially), and keep your edges trim; share your delights and disappointments. Who knows, you might win them over to this brand-new gardening adventure.

Eva Hoepfner lives near Toronto, where she "risked altering suburbia by killing the turf in the front yard and planting fruit, vegetables and ornamentals."

35

Chapter Four:
Alphabetical Ground Covers

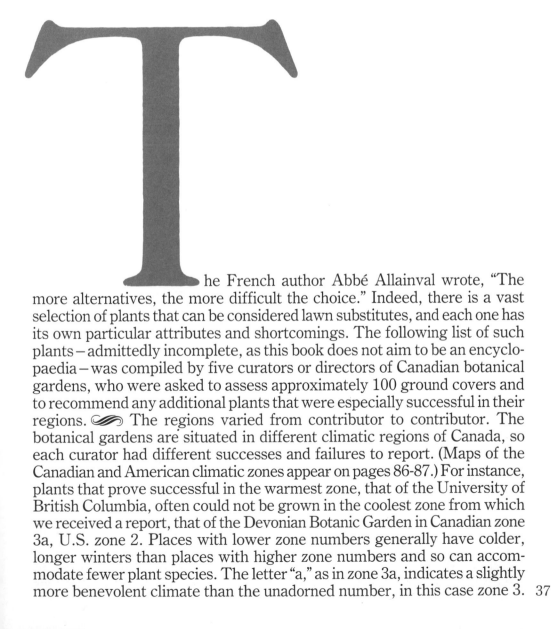

he French author Abbé Allainval wrote, "The more alternatives, the more difficult the choice." Indeed, there is a vast selection of plants that can be considered lawn substitutes, and each one has its own particular attributes and shortcomings. The following list of such plants – admittedly incomplete, as this book does not aim to be an encyclopaedia – was compiled by five curators or directors of Canadian botanical gardens, who were asked to assess approximately 100 ground covers and to recommend any additional plants that were especially successful in their regions. ᔕ The regions varied from contributor to contributor. The botanical gardens are situated in different climatic regions of Canada, so each curator had different successes and failures to report. (Maps of the Canadian and American climatic zones appear on pages 86-87.) For instance, plants that prove successful in the warmest zone, that of the University of British Columbia, often could not be grown in the coolest zone from which we received a report, that of the Devonian Botanic Garden in Canadian zone 3a, U.S. zone 2. Places with lower zone numbers generally have colder, longer winters than places with higher zone numbers and so can accommodate fewer plant species. The letter "a," as in zone 3a, indicates a slightly more benevolent climate than the unadorned number, in this case zone 3.

Therefore, although gardeners will find it useful (and sometimes entertaining) to read all the comments about any particular plant—not just climate but also personal preference is involved here—it will be most helpful at least at the outset, to take into consideration one's own climatic zone in judging whose comments are most relevant. As the just-mentioned example illustrates, there is little point in a gardener in the northern prairies buying plants recommended by Gerald Straley of Vancouver but found unable to survive by P.N.D. Seymour in Edmonton. You are well advised to heed the advice of botanists in the same climatic zone or a climatic zone with a lower number than your own. In alphabetical order, they are:

TC: Trevor Cole, curator, Dominion Arboretum, Ottawa Research Station, Ottawa, Ontario. Agriculture Canada climatic zone 5a; United States Department of Agriculture (USDA) zone 4.

BJ: Bernard Jackson, curator, Memorial University Botanical Garden, St. John's, Newfoundland. Agriculture Canada climatic zone 5b; USDA zone 5.

AP: Allen Paterson, director, Royal Botanical Gardens, Hamilton, Ontario. Agriculture Canada climatic zone 6b; USDA zone 6.

GS: Gerald B. Straley, research scientist and curator of collections, The Botanical Garden, University of British Columbia, Vancouver, British Columbia. Agriculture Canada climatic zone 9a; USDA zone 8.

PS: P. N. D. Seymour, director, Devonian Botanic Garden, Edmonton, Alberta. Agriculture Canada climatic zone 3a; USDA zone 2.

Achillea tomentosa

(woolly yarrow)

The genus *Achillea* includes many medicinal and ornamental plants, but the best for ground covering is the carpeting species *A. tomentosa*, with woolly, feathery, grey-green aromatic foliage and bright yellow summer flowers on stems 6 to 10 inches tall. Most yarrows, woolly or otherwise, prefer to grow in rich soil with good drainage in full sun. It is best to propagate by division; seed germinates poorly.

TC: It grows moderately fast and, if planted about 12 inches apart, should close in after three years or so.

BJ: The dwarf yarrows are temperamental in the Newfoundland area, doing fairly well in some gardens but failing in others. They do not seem to like our erratic winter weather and especially resent being covered with wet snow. The wild yarrow (*Achillea millefolium*), however, does well on poor but well-drained soils and has potential as a ground cover in areas where a natural effect is wanted. It is 1 to 3 feet tall with white or reddish flowers.

GS: *Achillea tomentosa* is very rarely grown in southwestern B.C., although the few plants seen here in sunny, well-drained locations look good. Remove the spent flower stalks—using a mower with blades set at a high level.

PS: *Achillea tomentosa* is not recommended for heavy soils, and it does well on sand at the Devonian Botanic Garden. Every three years, the young growth from the edges of clumps should be lifted and replanted. 'Rose Beauty' is a rapid spreader with showy, rose-pink flowers. It, too, needs replanting after three years.

Aegopodium podagraria

(goutweed; bishop's weed)

A little too vigorous for most situations, this hardy, coarse, fast-growing deciduous perennial forms 6-inch-deep mats of sharply toothed, ovate leaves in sun or shade. The white umbels of spring flowers are somewhat attractive, but the plants look best if faded flowers are removed. Goutweed self-sows readily and spreads by creeping rootstocks.

1:2

TC: There are a few situations where this plant is acceptable, such as in cement-locked beds where it cannot escape; generally, however, do not plant it, as it is most invasive. The roots travel below the soil surface, and it can even appear on the other side of a sidewalk.

BJ: This plant grows extremely well, especially in good soil, in sun or partial shade. It should be used only to cover the local garbage dump, never in the garden. The variety *variegatum* is nowhere near as rampant and can be used to advantage in areas where a single ground cover is required. Its variegated leaves can be particularly attractive in shady areas.

AP: A noxious weed, except in its variegated form – and even then, it is best contained by a curb, as it is in the Royal Botanical Gardens' parking medians, or planted where spread is unimportant. The variegated form may revert to the weedy species.

GS: Locally, it is called "ground elder" because the leaves resemble those of the shrub elderberry. The wild green form is a serious pest here, but the variegated form with a white leaf edge is showier and slightly less invasive.

PS: The species itself is very weedy and not worth growing, but the form *variegatum* is an excellent plant for dense cover in semishade on moist soils.

Ajuga reptans

(bugleweed)

A valuable but somewhat invasive ground cover, *Ajuga* spreads by above-ground runners, eventually becoming dense enough to exclude many weeds. The rosettes of green leaves, and especially the bronze or variegated-leaved forms, are neat and attractive, and the plant produces fat, 4-to-6-inch spikes of blue flowers. It responds well to good moist organic soil in partial shade, although it will grow in full sun as well. Propagate by division in spring or fall, and set plants 9 to 12 inches apart.

TC: The species itself makes an excellent cover for fairly wild areas where it may have to take occasional heavy traffic, such as under apple trees. In general, however, *Ajuga* is a bit invasive and can spread into lawns. The coloured forms, such as 'Gaiety' and 'Burgundy Glow,' are 39 more desirable in a formal area, but they spread more slowly. Discard any pieces that revert to the green form.

BJ: The 'Multicolor' cultivar has striking purple-and-golden foliage, while *variegata* has leaves splashed and edged with cream-yellow. All are worth growing.

1:2

AP: The bronze and variegated forms are most desirable.

GS: Although it can be a pest if it creeps into lawns, this is one of the best semi-deciduous (often evergreen in Vancouver) ground covers for filtered shade. The spikes of bright blue spring flowers (more rarely pink or white) contrast well when planted beneath flowering shrubs such as pink or white azaleas. This combination is used very well along the rhododendron walk at VanDusen Botanical Gardens in Vancouver.

PS: Tends to die out in patches, leaving isolated pieces to survive. Not a good ground cover in Edmonton.

Alchemilla mollis

(Lady's mantle)

The panicles of green-gold flowers are insignificant, but the crimped, deciduous green leaves of Lady's mantle are most attractive and add a somewhat unusual texture to the garden landscape. The plants form rounded clumps about a foot tall. They spread by creeping rootstocks and self-sow readily. Lady's mantle tolerates shade but not wet ground. Once established, it will easily smother most weeds.

TC: While it will make a sort of ground cover, *Alchemilla mollis* is most often grown as a specimen plant. It does well in semishade, and the greenish yellow flowers have a strange charm if you really look at them.

BJ: It has potential as a ground cover for poor soil in light shade. In full sun and good soil, it becomes too tall and lush to be used for this purpose.

1:4

GS: Very easily grown in Vancouver, it reseeds easily and is trouble-free. It is more often seen, however, as a specimen plant or in groups of plants used with perennials. Another species, *Alchemilla alpina*, is also seen in this area and is probably a better ground cover than *A. mollis*. The leaves are smaller, darker green above and silvery and silky beneath. The flowers are in smaller, elongated clusters.

PS: There are many *Alchemilla* species

40

that are good ground covers for spring and summer. They lose their leaves in winter.

Antennaria dioica

(pussytoes)

1:2

This North American native forms a tight 1-inch mat of rosettes of soft, grey hairy foliage. The white or pink daisylike flowers that bloom on 6-inch stems in summer are followed by fluffy seed heads. Plants are easily propagated from self-rooted pieces of creeping stems, and tiny plants will spring up from self-sown seeds. Set the plants about 9 inches apart, as they are slow to spread, and give them a site with good drainage in full sun.

TC: A wonderful ground cover for dry, sandy soils, but it does not grow well in wet places. It will take moderate traffic and is long-lived.

BJ: Newfoundland has a large number of native pussytoes. They grow admirably in gritty, well-drained soil. Many have attractive, silvery foliage and spread to form a low dense carpet. They are possibly best used along the edges of walkways where they can be readily admired but where foot traffic is not excessively heavy.

GS: A good perennial whose blooms, especially the pink forms, are moderately attractive but should be removed after flowering. The leaves usually remain over winter.

PS: Many *Antennaria* species grow on the prairies. All have silvery foliage and make excellent ground covers in the Edmonton area.

Anthemis nobilis or Chamaemelum nobile

(Roman chamomile)

1:1

Related to the annual herb French chamomile well known for its inclusion in salubrious teas, this perennial has foliage that is attractive, finely cut, aromatic and edible. The flowers are small, yellow-eyed white daisies on 12-inch stems. A low- 41 growing plant, it will spread fairly fast in sandy soils and full sun, making a good ground cover. Although it may be difficult to find plants, herb dealers usually offer seeds, and mature plants can be propagated by division. Plant 6 inches apart.

TC: The 'Treneague' variety is non-flowering and is occasionally used to make a lawn. It is not suitable for areas that get a lot of traffic, and it is of borderline hardiness in the Ottawa area.

BJ: Some species of this genus are inclined to be temperamental here in St. John's.

AP: Best clipped to prevent its flowering. 'Treneague' is a nonflowering form better for ground cover.

GS: Not seen in the Vancouver area, but I am not sure why. Maybe the coast is too wet in winter for it to grow well.

PS: Not hardy in the Edmonton area.

Arabis caucasica or A. albida

(rock cress)

Greyish tumbling growth hidden beneath a cloud of white or pink-purple spring flowers suits this 10-inch plant to the sort of small areas also preferred by *Aubrieta*, *Iberis* and *Aurinia*, with whom it often shares company. Given full sun and good drainage, each plant should cover about a square foot. The double forms must be propagated vegetatively, but others are easily grown from seed. Before seed is set, shear off the dead flower heads along with about a third of the foliage to ensure that the plants stay in good condition and bloom profusely.

TC: Not one of my favourite ground covers because unless it is cut back hard after flowering (which defeats the easy-care objective of ground covers), it tends to die out in the middle. Maybe close planting so that one plant could grow into the crown of the next would work.

BJ: I believe *Arabis alpina* to be more reliable in my area (St. John's). The cultivar 'Grandiflora' with large white flowers

1:1

and the variety *rosea* with rose-purple blooms both produce glorious splashes of colour. They are useful for hanging over walls, for edging walkways and as specimens in the rock garden or on scree.

GS: Good for rock crevices, for covering the edges of walls and for well-drained areas.

PS: Not reliably hardy in the Edmonton area.

Arctostaphylos uva-ursi

(bearberry; kinnikinnick)

This native evergreen ground cover produces dense, 6-to-10-inch carpets of small, shiny dark green leaves and sprays of fragrant pink flowers, followed by red berries, for year-round interest. Bearberry will grow in shade but does better in full sun, especially in a well-drained, acidic, gritty but organically rich soil. It is sometimes slow to establish, but once settled, it will expand by as much as 18 inches a season. One plant can easily cover a 5-foot circle.

TC: Good for hot sandy soils in full sun.

BJ: Rarely grown in the Newfoundland area and unavailable from the local commercial trade; however, it does have great potential for the home garden and can be ordered from mainland nurseries or propagated (slowly) from cuttings judiciously collected in the wild. It is difficult to induce it to flower and produce berries in my area.

AP: The new 'Vancouver Jade' is good.

GS: One of the best evergreen ground covers for sun or partial shade in acidic but well-drained soils, bearberry gives good cover quickly and is adaptable to a wide range of situations and climates. One problem is its susceptibility to leaf galls. Several cultivars are available. 'Vancouver Jade,' released from this botanical garden, is an especially vigorous, disease-resistant form.

1:1

PS: A native plant in the Edmonton region, although some forms, such as 'Wood's Red,' did not succeed here. Good in sun or shade.

Arenaria verna or Minuartia verna

(Irish-moss, sandwort)

Arenaria verna is a 3-inch-tall carpet-forming plant that looks like a moss but has tiny white starlike flowers. It grows in partial shade or full sun, although it may need watering in sun. There is a yellow-flowered form that requires full sun to keep its colour. The seed germinates readily, and the plants can be divided quite

easily. *A. verna* will grow in a variety of soils and tolerates light foot traffic.

1:1

TC: Slow-growing; this is a ground cover for small spaces. It can be planted between paving stones in areas that are not heavily used.

BJ: Grows well in Newfoundland. It is a useful ground cover between flagstones or where a very low mat-forming plant is required. There is a popular variety, *aurea*, with yellow-green leaves.

AP: It is good between stones but will take little wear. The golden-leaved form is good.

GS: Not often used in the Vancouver region, except in botanical gardens.

PS: There are several *Arenaria* species in cultivation, none of which we would recommend for the Edmonton area as ground covers.

Armeria maritima or A. vulgaris

(thrift, sea-pink)

This grasslike evergreen forms tight tussocks of 2- to-10-inch-long, dark green

43

leaves and bears pink or white, ball-like flowers in papery calyxes that are held high above the leaves for a long time. The clumps spread to about 15 inches wide. Adaptable to a wide range of conditions, thrift fares best in full sun and well-drained soil. As its common name suggests, it is tolerant of salt spray. Propagate by division or from seed.

1:3

TC: A mounding plant that spreads slowly and dies out in the centre. This is often recommended as a ground cover, but I think it leaves a lot to be desired, although it is very pretty in flower, and the form is good at first.

BJ: Native to the St. John's area, but the cultivated varieties are far superior. I do not consider it a ground cover, but it is a good specimen in rock gardens or as an edging for a formal bed. The less common white-flowered variety is worth having, if you can obtain it.

AP: 'Beespink' is a bright cultivar.

GS: Established clumps are dense enough to exclude weeds. It makes good cover for small areas or when mixed with other spreading plants or those with bold foliage, such as *Bergenia*.

PS: Good in a sunny location but tends to be short-lived.

Artemisia spp

(wormwood)

Grown for their beautiful, dissected silvery foliage rather than for their inconspicuous flowers, the artemisias include several medicinal herbs and many ornamentals. Give them good drainage in full sun; they will tolerate some shade, but will become leggy and the foliage will be greener. One of the best for ground cover is *Artemisia schmidtiana nana*, called 'Silver Mound,' which forms 12-inch-wide tussocks of 8-inch-tall foliage. Some species can be grown from seed, but others do not produce seeds and must be propagated asexually. Buy plants and then divide or take cuttings.

TC: One member of the genus *Artemisia* is the native sagebrush, so the plants are obviously well suited to dry, sunny sites. Some cultivars, such as 'Silver Mound,' increase very slowly, while others like *A. pontica* will spread rapidly and can even grow into the lawn.

1:12

BJ: I do not consider them ground covers, certainly not in the Newfoundland area. If they grow in full sun and a lean soil, however, they form nice, compact, tidy clumps that add great interest to a rock garden. They are improved by a light midsummer shearing to encourage dense new growth and to discourage the production of flowers. Since artemisias are often affected by winter dieback, a careful though heavy spring shearing may be required. They need a well-drained site, but the soil around their roots should never dry out. 'Silver Mound' is the most common dwarf species in my area.

AP: *Artemisia schmidtiana nana* forms a low ground cover, a wide dome of silver filigree with insignificant yellow flowers. *A. stellerana* is bigger in all its parts but also fairly low, growing to about 1 foot.

GS: *Artemisia stellerana* is good in sunny locations here in Vancouver and tolerates sandy soil. The tall spikes of flowers are not attractive, and the plant looks best if sheared back when the flower spikes begin growing.

PS: 'Silver Mound' is an excellent ground cover for warm sunny areas. It is comparatively slow-growing but better on well-drained soil. *Artemisia ludoviciana albula*, called 'Silver King,' is a 20-inch plant with rather rank silvery foliage. It spreads rapidly into large clumps and is good in a hot dry location.

Asarum spp

(wild ginger)

The wild gingers receive their name not from a kinship with the culinary plant but from their gingerlike fragrance. Typical woodland plants, they do best in shady, moist, humus-rich soil, where they spread by creeping rootstocks. The broad, heart-shaped leaves on 7-to-10-inch stems are attractive in summer, but most species die back in winter. Inconspicuous, reddish brown urn-shaped flowers are borne near ground level in late spring. Propagate by division.

TC: A good group of plants for growing in the shade of taller shrubs. The native ginger, or Canada snakeroot (*Asarum*

canadense), in particular will spread slowly and choke out weeds. The others do not make such good ground covers.

1:6

AP: *Asarum canadense* and *A. caudatum* are deciduous, with soft, rounded leaves. They accept full shade and summer drought. *A. europaeum* has smaller, circular, shiny evergreen leaves. It may be less cold-tolerant but survives under a snow cover. Give it full shade or half sun.

GS: *Asarum caudatum*, our native species, is most often seen in Vancouver. Slugs are a problem. The evergreen *A. europaeum* is the best, but it is not generally available.

PS: *Asarum canadense* and *A. caudatum* have not been tried at the botanical garden here in Edmonton. *A. europaeum* grows slowly on damp soil but never really looks happy.

Astilbe chinensis pumila

(dwarf Chinese false spirea)

Like other astilbes, this cultivar is best identified by its erect, showy spikes of airy

45

flowers. It is smaller in all its parts than the usual garden astilbes but also has fernlike leaves and produces its mauve-pink flowers in late summer and autumn. Easily propagated by division, it prefers a moist but well-drained, gritty soil with a fair amount of incorporated organic matter.

TC: All the astilbes are good plants for light shade and moist sites, but this species spreads slowly by underground runners and thus is well suited to use as a ground cover.

1:8

BJ: A delightful, creeping plant with potential as a ground cover for small areas. Unfortunately, our St. John's summer is sometimes too short to guarantee flowering. The leaves are very susceptible to early-fall or late-spring frosts, but the plant survives this damage. Planting in full sun in an airy site away from low-lying areas is best here. It has to be kept well weeded.

AP: It can be grown in half shade.

GS: For moist soils in full sun, this is a good but slowly spreading cover. It is easily grown in southwestern British Columbia but not generally available.

PS: Very slow-growing in the Edmonton area and does not form an attractive plant.

Aubrieta spp

(false rock cress; stonecress)

1:1

This common rock garden plant forms foot-wide 2-to-6-inch mats of greyish foliage covered in spring with flowers that are typically lavender but sometimes white, purple or reddish. For quick effect, set plants 6 inches apart, but a 12-inch spacing will fill in fairly rapidly. The named forms are propagated vegetatively—it is fine to use seed for the rest. Plant *Aubrieta* in full sun in well-drained soil.

TC: This is not as liable to centre die-back as *Arabis*, and thus is preferable, but not for use in areas that receive any foot traffic. It is easy to raise from seed if you need many plants or from cuttings to increase a particular colour.

BJ: Though notoriously easy to grow in Britain, this plant performs erratically in the St. John's area. A few gardens have nice, respectable clumps, while other clumps, mine included, fail miserably. The plant certainly does not like being covered with the wet, slushy snow that is often part of our winters, so it is of no value as a ground cover here. It is, how-

46

ever, a pretty rock garden plant easily propagated from seed, so well worth trying if you are of a philosophical nature.

GS: *Aubrieta deltoidea* is best used in rock crevices and above walls, over which it can cascade. It is often used with *Arabis* and *Aurinia*. A variegated form with yellow and green foliage is especially attractive. *Aubrieta* is widely used here to cover small areas.

PS: Not reliable in the Edmonton area; survives winter only occasionally.

Aurinia saxatilis or Alyssum saxatile

(basket-of-gold)

This herbaceous perennial grows about 6 inches tall and has attractive, 2-to-5-inch-long silvery leaves. The bright yellow flower clusters that suggest its common name are produced in spring and sometimes again later on. Mature plants self-sow fairly readily, and basket-of-gold is easily grown from seed. Set plants 10 to 12 inches apart in full sun on good-quality, well-drained soil. Start new plants every few years as the older ones become woody and less attractive.

TC: This is one of the most common rock plants, since it seeds itself and can choke out most other plants – characteristics that make it an excellent ground cover. Mowing after flowering (with blades set high) will cut down on seed production.

BJ: Does well in the St. John's area but can suffer winter damage, especially if covered for prolonged periods with wet, slushy snow. It benefits from planting out of the wind and from a fairly heavy shearing immediately after flowering. *Aurinia saxatilis compactum* is a dwarf and more compact variety that could be used as a ground cover.

AP: The pale yellow form, *citrina*, is easier to place amongst other plants. Clip back after flowering to encourage summer leaves.

GS: One of the most common spring-flowering perennials, usually used in small areas. A few flowers may be produced during mild winters. *Alyssum maritimum* has neater, more compact growth than the similar, more widely used *A. saxatile*.

1:2

PS: A short-lived perennial in the Edmonton area but will resow itself each year. Useful when grown as individual plants but not really suitable as a ground cover.

Bergenia cordifolia

(giant rockfoil; heartleaf bergenia)

Broad, glossy, leathery leaves that turn coppery in winter distinguish this evergreen perennial. The plants have thick rootstocks from which they develop into large low clumps or colonies about 20 inches tall. Spikes of attractive pink, white or purplish flowers are borne above the leaves in spring. Bergenias will grow in sun or shade and seem to prefer rich, 47 moist, well-drained soil. Propagate by division.

TC: The large evergreen leaves make this a good ground cover. In areas with cold winters and little snow cover, the foliage can be badly frost-damaged, but the plant quickly produces new leaves. There are a few different species and hybrids to extend the flowering season – if you can find them.

BJ: Flowering in the Newfoundland area is erratic and often disappointing (possibly due to our winters). *Bergenia* can look cumbersome and inappropriate if not placed carefully but can be very effective and beautiful beneath deciduous trees. It is sometimes slow to settle in a new site but, once happy, will increase its clump size admirably.

1:6

AP: I recommend the named forms such as 'Silberlicht' ('Silverlight'), 'Ballawley,' 'Schmidtii' and such.

GS: Very common in the Vancouver area and appropriate to mix with other ground covers for contrast.

PS: A good general ground cover for semishade to full sun; widely grown in the

48

Edmonton region. New varieties do not seem as hardy.

Calluna vulgaris

(Scottish heather)

1:2

The plant that colours the Scottish Highlands, this low shrub has tiny overlapping leaves and spikes of small bell-shaped single or double flowers of white, pink or purple in late summer and autumn. There are dozens of named varieties from 3 to 24 inches tall, in a range of flower and foliage colours. Easily grown from 1-inch cuttings in a mixture of sand and peat, heather also multiplies fairly readily from self-sown seed; plant about 18 inches apart and be patient. Heather grows best in a well-drained mixture of sand, peat and leaf mould that is never allowed to dry out, but it will tolerate a variety of soils, provided they are free of lime; it responds to an annual topdressing of shredded peat. Shear off the old flower heads annually, but leave them until spring so they will help trap the snow and protect the roots from frost damage; a good snow cover in winter is a definite advantage in colder areas.

TC: Given the right conditions, heather makes an ideal ground cover. An acidic soil, shade during the heat of the day and either a minimum winter temperature of minus 4 degrees F or a reliable snow cover are needed for this plant to thrive. Hardiness varies with the variety, so you may have to experiment.

BJ: Our acidic soil and damp climate in the St. John's area seem perfectly suited to this delightful, exciting group of plants that make ideal ground covers and, once established, smother out almost any type of weed.

GS: Excellent low-spreading evergreens that may be sheared back in spring or just after bloom to encourage dense growth. There are many varieties grown here in Vancouver with green to grey, gold or even pink or orange foliage with white to pink or mauve flowers. There is a particularly fine collection in the Heather Garden at VanDusen Botanical Gardens in Vancouver.

PS: In the Edmonton area, the plant needs shelter from the early-morning sun and bears little resemblance to the vigorous plant of milder climates. It is not a good ground cover here.

Cerastium tomentosum

(snow-in-summer)

Rampant mats of grey foliage grow about 9 inches tall and, as the common name suggests, produce many white flowers in spring or summer. A tough plant, snow-in-summer will tolerate almost any soil, eventually covering an area of about 9 square feet by rooting from stems that extend along the ground and then turn upward. Propagate by seeds, cuttings or division, setting plants 1 or 2 feet apart in full sun.

TC: A most invasive plant that can even

crowd out basket-of-gold. You must be fanatical about mowing or clipping off the seed heads if it is not to take over *everywhere*. With care, however, it is an excellent ground cover. The closely related *Cerastium lanatum* (woolly snow-in-summer) is a lower-growing, less invasive form but is not easy to find.

BJ: I feel that it has the potential of becoming a garden pest of note and would not allow it into a garden of mine.

1:2

AP: *Cerastium tomentosum* is not to be mixed with delicate alpines.

GS: Good and easy. Most often seen in rock crevices or cascading over walls with *Aubrieta*, *Arabis* and *Aurinia*. Not strong enough to compete with many weeds.

PS: Best in sunny locations, where it forms large mats.

Clematis tangutica

(golden clematis)

A coarse hardy clematis, whose nodding, bright yellow, 3-inch flowers resemble lemon peels. The flowers are followed by fluffy white seed heads. The vines, which climb, carpet stumps and stones or spread over the ground, grow about 12 feet long and flower the first season from seed. Plant *Clematis tangutica* in rich, well-drained soil in shade or sun.

BJ: If you want an imaginative, unusual

49

ground cover, try this. It grows well for me if protected from the wind and is particularly good for trailing and running over a not-too-steep bankside in partial shade. Use it for the special site where you and your friends can give it the admiration it deserves.

1:6

PS: We use it as a ground cover in the rock garden, where it is very striking. It grows into low mounds and spreads around the area.

Clintonia borealis

(bluebead lily)

Named for its handsome umbels of blue berries in autumn, this eastern North American native grows 6 to 8 inches tall in cool, moist woods — even in deep shade. It has broad, dark green, shiny leaves and nodding green-and-yellow flowers, which are borne above the leaves in late spring. The bluebead lily spreads into a carpet by creeping rhizomes that divide at the nodes to form additional plants. Grow from plants, rhizomes or seeds acquired from wildflower sources. It matures extremely

slowly from seed, sometimes taking several years to flower.

1:3

BJ: This beautiful woodland plant can quickly cover a suitable site beneath the dappled shade of deciduous or mixed trees. It requires moist, acidic, organic soil and seems to prefer a fairly high humidity. If happy, it will spread quite rapidly. Best suited to a naturalistic garden.

Convallaria majalis

(lily-of-the-valley)

Known best for its sweetly fragrant, waxy, bell-like flowers, lily-of-the-valley is also an admirable ground cover for certain situations. Pairs of bright green, deciduous, 8-inch-tall leaves push through purple sheaths in April. The white (sometimes pinkish) flowers follow in May, and poisonous red berries appear by August. Lily-of-the-valley prefers light, humus-rich soils that are never allowed to dry out, but will grow quite well in a variety of other soils, even those with poor drainage. The plant multiplies rapidly by underground rhizomes and is easily divided for transplanting in early fall. Plant 7 inches apart. A light fall mulch of well-rotted leaf mould will protect the roots from exposure caused by heavy rain and frost heave.

TC: A partly shaded site and poor soil are ideal for lily-of-the-valley. It can spread into lawns and other planted areas, but since the runners are fairly shallow, a barrier of 6-inch, heavy-gauge plastic set vertically into the soil will contain it nicely.

1:3

BJ: A favourite old ground cover that can stand considerable sunlight but is much better growing in the shade of deciduous trees.

AP: Can be overly robust in moist soil.

GS: Often used to cover small areas in shade.

PS: Excellent deciduous ground cover for shady areas or on the north side of a house. A very reliable, hardy plant.

Cornus canadensis

(bunchberry)

Related to the dogwood tree, this 3-to-6-inch-tall plant produces the same type of flower in miniature in spring or summer, followed in fall by large, round clumps of brilliant scarlet berries. The showy leaves are broad and whorled. Bunchberry spreads rapidly by rhizome in suitably shady areas in moist, acidic soils and can become a nuisance if allowed to overcome less vigorous plants. Propagate by division, and set plants a foot apart.

TC: While this is often recommended as a ground cover, I have never seen a stand that was thick enough to shade out weeds. In theory, however, its habit is ideal, and it grows best in light shade, which makes it perfect for use beneath shrubs, but be prepared to weed at least once each summer to remove that year's crop of dandelion seedlings.

BJ: A beautiful native ground cover for use in acidic, organically rich soils. It can grow in unbelievably exposed locations, but to form a good thick carpet, it needs the shade and atmospheric humidity of tree and shrub growth. It makes a good companion for ferns and is particularly effective if allowed to form large informal drifts in a naturalistic garden.

AP: Bunchberry is very appealing when interspersed with rhododendrons and heathers.

1:6

GS: For shaded situations and in acidic, peaty soils, this is a very good ground cover, although it is fairly slow to become established. Should be used here (Vancouver) more often than it is.

PS: This common poplar-woodlands ground cover seems difficult to establish in gardens, where I have seen it only once. With perseverance, it might be induced to form a mat in a shady area.

Cornus sericea

(red osier dogwood)

1:2

A dogwood-tree relative, this species is a 5-to-7-foot shrub available in several varieties, such as *flaviramea*, with yellow twigs. It will grow in sun and shade in almost any soil with reasonable organic content. The branches can be pruned to the ground every three or four years to make the plants denser and more colourful. Propagate by division and plant 4 feet apart. The variety *kelseyi*, the Kelsey dogwood, is a smaller form that grows less than 2 feet tall.

TC: In wet areas, such as are found on many cottage lots, the red osier will make a first-class ground cover. It spreads by underground runners and forms a dense thicket. It is particularly attractive during the winter, when its bright red bark is visible.

Coronilla varia

(crown vetch)

Because it is a legume, a member of the pea family, crown vetch has roots that are capable of fixing their own nitrogen and enhancing soil quality. The plant's drought resistance, its 2-foot, robust, bushy growth, its sprays of pink flowers in early summer and its ability to spread by underground runners have made it popular for use on roadside banks, where it holds the soil in place and needs little or no maintenance. It dies back in winter. Broadcast seed or set plants 2 feet apart in full sun or partial shade.

1:2

TC: Widely used as a roadside ground cover, but to my mind, crown vetch is a bit coarse for all but the larger gardens. In

Ottawa, it seems to be a bit on the borderline of hardiness, and in exposed locations, it often dies out during harsh winters. 'Penngift' is a superior form but not quite as hardy as the species.

BJ: A very unreliable plant in Newfoundland.

AP: Good for soil conservation on banks but probably too aggressive for small gardens.

GS: Good mixed with *Lotus corniculatus* among tall grasses for a rough, irregular cover on banks.

PS: Not reliably hardy in the Edmonton area.

Cotoneaster spp

(rock spray, cotoneaster)

This genus includes mainly evergreen shrubs with white or pinkish flowers that are followed by scarlet berries. Depending on species, plants may reach 1 to 4 feet in height and spread 4 to 10 feet, the spreading forms rooting wherever their branches touch the ground. Propagate by division, or layer the shoots in fall. All species require full sun.

TC: Many of the spreading and semi-upright cotoneasters make ideal ground covers, provided the gardener is willing to hoe and weed for the first few years. Among the best are creeping rock spray (*Cotoneaster horizontalis*), a real ground-hugger; Skogholm cotoneaster (*C. dammeri* 'Skogholm'), taller with white flowers that are followed by red berries; and the species itself, *C. dammeri*, the bearberry cotoneaster, which is taller still at 18 inches.

BJ: The prostrate cotoneasters make good ground covers and are particularly effective when used to cover bare slopes. In the St. John's area, two good ones are *Cotoneaster horizontalis* and *C. adpressus praecox*. The bearberry cotoneaster (*C. dammeri*) is a superb ground cover but somewhat tender unless grown where a deep snow cover is assured.

AP: The best kinds include *Cotoneaster dammeri*, which is completely flat; *C. salicifolius repens*, with long leaves and a spray habit; the cultivar 'Skogholm,' which is very robust for large areas, and

1:3

C. horizontalis, which is deciduous with a fish-bone growth habit and good fall colour.

GS: Cotoneasters are among the best shrubby ground covers for coastal British Columbia. A number of species and cultivars, including *Cotoneaster adpressus*, *C. macrophyllus*, *C. dammeri* and *C. horizontalis*, are often used for large commercial plantings.

PS: The dwarf spreading cotoneaster species are not hardy in the Edmonton region.

Cytisus spp, Genista spp

(broom)

Members of the pea family, brooms for ground covering belong to two very simi- 53 lar genera that comprise woody shrubs with switchlike branches and pea flowers in spring or summer. *Genista pilosa* is a 4-to-12-inch evergreen that roots as it spreads, forming dense undulating mounds of small leaves on arching grey-green stems covered with bright yellow flowers in late spring or early summer. It spreads about 3 feet wide. Give brooms full sun, slightly acidic soil and excellent drainage. They may be propagated by layering or by cuttings started in early spring.

1:2

TC: There are two brooms that I particularly recommend: the double form of Dyer's greenweed (*Genista tinctoria* 'Plena'), a 12-inch mat-forming plant covered with yellow flowers in spring; and a new introduction from the University of British Columbia, 'Vancouver Gold,' a very prostrate, free-flowering plant. Both will do well in full sun and light sandy soils. Others that can be used include the prostrate broom (*Cytisus decumbens*) and the silky-leaved woodwaxen (*G. pilosa*),

both of which grow about 2 feet tall.

BJ: Preliminary evidence suggests that in Newfoundland *Cytisus* is far too tender and unreliable to warrant the effort. *Genista*, a favourite of visitors to our botanical garden, has great potential for small, important sites. New-wood cuttings root quite easily in a mixture of peat and sand during late summer or early fall.

AP: Frost hardiness needs consideration in the East, but *Cytisus beanii* and *C. kewensis* are worth considering. I recommend *Genista pilosa* 'Vancouver Gold.'

GS: *Cytisus multiflorus* is common on the West Coast and is used to a limited degree as a very tall (3-to-6-foot) cover for large bank and berm plantings, if planted close together, but brooms are usually grown as specimen plants. White to yellow flowers are strongly perfumed and cause hay fever symptoms in many people.

PS: *Cytisus* species such as *kewensis* are not hardy. Both *C. hirsutus* and *C. ratisbonensis* form 2-foot plants in hot dry areas; both have small yellow pealike flowers and seed freely. They can be cut back every two or three years. There are several *Genista* species and cultivars grown in the Edmonton area. Especially good is the new University of British Columbia Botanical Garden cultivar of *G. pilosa* 'Vancouver Gold.'

Dianthus spp

(pinks)

There are many species of pinks, popular garden plants that produce tussocks of narrow, grey-green spikelike leaves and clove-scented single or double flowers in colours ranging from white to·dark pink. Purchased or grown from seed, plants used for ground cover should be spaced about 18 inches apart if you are not in a rush, 12 inches apart for quick effect. Plant pinks in full sun and well-drained soil. Propagate by seed or by cuttings.

TC: Many pinks are easy to raise from

1:2

seed, which will often give some variation in flower colour. Read the seed catalogues carefully, as some, such as the alpine pink, are quite small and should grow only 9 inches apart.

BJ: Not considered an important ground cover, but some dwarf species could be used to cover small sites.

AP: Look especially for old-fashioned scented forms such as 'Mrs. Sinkins' and 'Doris.'

GS: Attractive year-round, but not usually vigorous enough to compete with grasses and weeds. Often used to cover small areas or to fill spaces in rock walls.

PS: *Dianthus deltoides* forms large mats of light green leaves and has masses of small red flowers. For longer life, remove the seed heads. Self-sown seedlings appear frequently.

Duchesnea indica

(Indian, false or mock strawberry)

A perennial similar to the wild strawberry, although its leaves are thinner and smaller, the plant is hardier, the flowers are yellow, and the fruit is inedible. Like a strawberry, it spreads by runners. Propagate by seed or by division. In a sunny location, plant 12 inches apart in light, humus-rich soil.

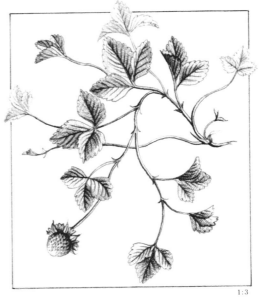

1:3

TC: A native of India, *Duchesnea* can be invasive if planted in good soil. It needs full sun and will withstand some foot traffic.

AP: Beastly tasting fruit.

PS: Easy in sun and partial shade. No serious insect or disease problems are known.

Epimedium spp

(bishop's hat, barrenwort)

These interesting plants are easy to identify, as one side of the leaf has a larger lobe than the other where the leaf joins the stem. In late spring, graceful racemes of small spurred flowers appear, tucked in among the leaves, in shades of white, pink, red or orange. The elegant, pink-flushed compound leaves are very attractive too, and their colour changes with the seasons. *Epimedium* will take full

55

shade but, in any situation, should be protected from the midday sun. In a well-drained, humus-rich, moisture-retentive soil, it spreads slowly by rhizome and grows 9 to 12 inches tall. Propagate by division and plant *Epimedium* 12 to 18 inches apart.

TC: A very distinctive plant, often with a reddish bronze tinge to the leaves.

BJ: I have never seen it used as a ground cover here in St. John's; however, it is well worth growing in small, irregular clumps in the flower garden. In my area, the old stems and leaves should be left to help trap snow, but be sure to cut them off early in spring before the plant starts growing.

GS: Very commonly seen in the Vancouver area, where several species are used to cover small areas in woodland gardens. The partially evergreen foliage should be sheared back in early spring just before new growth emerges. It burns in full sun.

1:4

PS: Here in Edmonton, *Epimedium* grows in damp semishaded areas. It does not form a thick cover as it does in milder climates, so it is interesting for the specialist but not recommended as a ground cover.

Erica carnea

(spring heath, heather)

1:1

Similar to *Calluna* but with smaller leaves and a narrower range of forms, these lower (usually 1 foot tall or less) evergreen shrubs also require acidic, leafy soil. The foliage is green or bronze ('Vivelii'). Sprays of white, pink or rosy red flower buds set in late summer and remain on the plant all winter to open in the early spring. Clip the flowers after blooming, and at the same time, top-dress the soil with a half-inch layer of compost. Heath is capable of smothering new weed growth, so once established, it requires little attention. It is particularly useful because it will tolerate considerable salt spray, air pollution and heavy shade, though it prefers at least half sun. Heath is easily propagated by layering or from 1-inch cuttings taken in late summer.

TC: Requires similar conditions and spacing to *Calluna* but is generally not quite as hardy. Try planting small-flowered crocus bulbs through it.

BJ: A very beautiful ground cover for special areas. Many cultivars are available from specialist nurseries, and 'King George,' 'Springwood Pink' and 'Springwood White' have proved particularly good here in St. John's. A deep, reliable snow cover is a definite advantage in growing this plant in cold areas.

GS: Excellent for growing with *Calluna vulgaris* in peaty, moist soils in full sun. Its outstanding feature is that it flowers in winter in Vancouver. There are many different forms grown here, an ideal climate for heaths and heathers.

PS: Does not form an adequate ground cover in Edmonton's climate.

Euonymus fortunei

(euonymus, wintercreeper)

A robust evergreen creeper or climber with leathery round leaves that may be green, variegated and, in winter, bronze. The inconspicuous and infrequent greenish flowers are succeeded by orange seeds in cream husks. *Euonymus* will climb if there is anything to cling to and spreads by trailing stems that root where they touch the ground. One plant will cover about 4 square feet and will make a ground cover 2 inches to 2 feet deep, depending on cultivar. Plants propagated by division, layering or cuttings should be set about 2 feet apart in any soil in shade or sun.

TC: Among many forms introduced in recent years are varieties with green-and-yellow and green-and-white leaves. These do not spread as rapidly as the older species and need more sun. In areas warmer than Canadian climatic zone 5, wintercreeper will also climb and become a wall cover. The named cultivars in particular are fairly slow-growing, so be prepared to weed by hand for several years. They will do well in sun or partial shade. *Euonymus* plants with plain green foliage are able to tolerate more shady locations.

1:2

BJ: Not very often seen in St. John's; possibly unreliable except where the snow cover is good.

AP: The variety *minimus* is the best small-leaved cover.

GS: Not very common in Vancouver, probably just because there are so many other ground covers that can be grown here.

PS: Not hardy in the Edmonton area.

Ferns

There may be more than 6,000 species of ferns — relatively primitive, spore-producing plants that are most appreciated in the garden for their graceful, luxurious foliage and their tolerance of shade and moist soil. No ferns do well, however, in 57 standing water or clay soil, and they tolerate little wind. Propagate them by division, and plant them 1 to 2 feet apart, depending on species.

1:8

TC: Ferns make good ground covers, provided the soil is enriched with humus before planting. One of the most useful is the ostrich fern (*Matteuccia struthiopteris*), which spreads by underground runners and soon makes a dense mat. This is the source of edible fiddleheads, which can be harvested in early spring after the plants have become established. The spores are produced on separate spikes rather than on the backs of the fronds, which can be left for winter display or cut for dried arrangements. A good ground cover, shown above, is the sensitive fern (*Onoclea sensibilis*), a lower-growing species (30 inches) with fronds that are not finely divided. It gets its name from its sensitivity to frost: the foliage is killed as soon as the temperature drops to freezing.

BJ: Many beautiful native ferns are easy to grow if given rich, moisture-retentive organic soil in light shade. They look best in natural landscaping but have a subtle beauty wherever they occur. A good ground cover where there is no foot traffic.

AP: A wide range of invaluable ground covers for shade and moist positions, including *Dryopteris* spp, *Matteuccia* spp and the sensitive fern.

GS: Some of the rhizomatous ferns, such as bracken (*Pteridium aquilinum*), are too invasive for anything but the largest areas. Clumped ones, especially the evergreen *Dryopteris* or *Polystichum* species, can be used as large ground covers if planted close together in shaded situations. Ferns are probably best used in groups to break the lines of flatter shade ground covers.

PS: *Matteuccia struthiopteris* grows about 2 feet tall and is a good ground cover in semishade. It spreads quite quickly and evenly.

Fragaria chiloensis

(wild strawberry)

Native from Alaska to South America, this is one of the parents of the cultivated strawberry. It, too, has the typical running strawberry habit that creates dense evergreen mats of shiny, dark green trifoliate leaves. Beautiful when its white flowers appear in spring, it later bears small but delicious fruits. Grow it in sun on well-drained soil. Propagate by seed or by division, setting plants 2 feet apart.

BJ: Wild strawberries make a delightful, almost indestructible ground cover. They cannot dominate certain grasses and weeds, so some maintenance is suggested. They seem to be more robust if grown in acidic, poor soil in full sun.

AP: *Fragaria vesca* is similar, and there is a white-fruited form.

GS: This is an adaptable evergreen for a wide range of conditions, but it is not

1:2

Heads of airy, white flowers and very fine, whorled, dark green foliage on arching 6- to-12-inch stems make this an attractive low plant for shade. A robust colonizer, it is nevertheless small and delicate in habit and is not strong enough for foot traffic. Propagate by division in fall. Sweet woodruff self-sows freely.

TC: It seems to thrive in even the darkest places, although most authorities recommend it for half shade. It spreads better than the more frequently recommended *Pachysandra*.

AP: This is good under trees in full shade, and it is aromatic when dried.

GS: Excellent for shade in moist soil, it is tolerant of sun but burns and then looks chlorotic (yellow or blanched).

PS: We have one plant but not enough experience with it to recommend it as a ground cover.

Gaultheria procumbens

(wintergreen)

A medicinal herb whose leaves make a fragrant tea, wintergreen is an evergreen, 6-inch (or lower) ground cover that spreads by underground runners. The dark green, shiny foliage turns purple in winter, and the white or pinkish bell-shaped flowers are followed by tasty, brilliant scarlet berries. Propagate by division, and set plants 6 inches apart in moist, acidic soil in light shade or sun.

TC: Although this native plant makes a loose mat in woodlands, it has not been very successful as a ground cover in Ottawa. It is difficult to transplant and seldom grows well enough to keep down weeds. Given an acidic soil, it would probably do better.

BJ: A very rare native plant in Newfoundland, this is a beautiful little evergreen ground cover that should be tried by all serious gardeners. My hope is that *Gaultheria* will soon become available in local nurseries.

GS: One of my favourite evergreen

used as much as it should be. It is very tolerant of salt spray and sandy soils. The University of British Columbia Botanical Garden is evaluating a number of clones for possible commercial introduction as ground covers.

PS: Has not been tried in the Edmonton area.

Galium odoratum, Asperula odorata

(sweet woodruff)

1:2

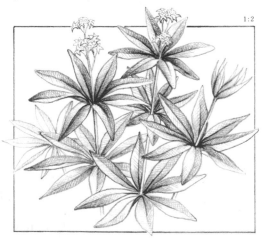

59

1:1

in flower. It forms a dense mound of foliage with flowers that vary from blue-mauve to white, pink and purple. Remove the flower heads from single-flowered varieties or they will self-seed and come up where they are not wanted. The double-flowered forms do not set seed.

1:1

ground covers for light shade or fairly sunny spots.

PS: I know of only one planting of *Gaultheria* in Edmonton, and it is inclined to make a rather thin ground cover in a shaded area.

Geranium spp

(cranesbill)

Unlike the tender, cultivated pelargoniums usually called geraniums, the true geraniums are hardy plants with lobed or divided leaves and small pink or purplish flowers. Some cranesbills spread by rhizomes and form mounds of sweetly scented foliage a few inches to several feet tall, depending on species. Propagate by seeds and root division.

BJ: *Geranium macrorrhizum* forms a dense, medium-height ground cover of particular value for its lovely russet leaves in fall. It grows well in good soil in full sun. Plants spaced 12 to 18 inches apart will soon grow together to create an impressive bed.

AP: Consider *Geranium sanguineum*, above, *G. tuberosum* and *G. psilostemon*.

PS: *Geranium sanguineum* is a low-growing (to 8 inches), dense, magenta-flowered plant. *G. pratense* grows up to 3 feet tall and up to 18 inches wide when

Grasses

Members of the family Gramineae, grasses — including edible, lawn, weedy and ornamental species — comprise a wide range of mainly tussock-forming plants. Most are best suited to well-drained soil in sun and are best propagated by seed or by division.

TC: The majority of ornamental grasses have a clumplike habit of growth and thus

1:10

stems should be removed to keep it looking presentable.

PS: *Phalaris arundinacea picta* forms lush, thick 30-inch-tall clumps of narrow green-and-white-striped foliage and is a good dense ground cover that prefers moist soil. *Holcus mollis albovariegatus* is similar but smaller—about a foot tall—a nice neat grass.

Hedera helix

(ivy)

1:6

are not very suitable for use as ground covers. In wild areas or on difficult-to-maintain slopes, however, the variegated gardener's garters, or canary grass (*Phalaris arundinacea picta*), can be put to good use. This variety, shown above, which grows as tall as 6 feet, spreads by underground runners and can become invasive in the perennial garden, but it is good as a ground cover.

AP: *Phalaris arundinacea picta* spreads well. Wild rye (*Elymus glaucus*) is robust with blue leaves.

GS: *Phalaris arundinacea picta* is a low, irregularly mounded grass sometimes cultivated here in Vancouver. It is easily grown and tends to be invasive. Blue fescue (*Festuca ovina glauca*) is a nice tufted grass with very blue, needlelike blades. It looks best if planted in individual tufts and must be replanted every few years to retain the compact clumps. The flowering

Most familiar as a climber of trees and walls, ivy also makes a fine, evergreen 6-to-12-inch-deep ground cover that spreads rapidly. Several cultivars with diverse leaf sizes and shapes are available. Tolerant of both fairly dark shade and full sun, ivy should be grown on well-drained soil. Propagate in spring or fall by cuttings 61 planted 12 inches apart.

TC: English ivy is hardy only in the warmest parts of the country. Baltic ivy is hardier and will survive to minus 4 degrees F, but it does not seem to make as thick a mat. Both do best in a shady situation and should be protected from the winter sun.

BJ: Ivy forms a dense, rather monotonous carpet in either sun or deep shade and does well as a ground cover in my area (St. John's), provided it is protected from our incessant winds and is covered with snow in winter. It will grow in a variety of soils but appears to do best here in a good clay loam.

AP: An invaluable evergreen cover for shade. Golden ('Gold Heart') and variegated ('Glacier') forms exist. The *baltica* variety is perhaps the hardiest.

GS: Commonly naturalized around southwestern British Columbia, this is the best woody vine used as a ground cover. The small-leaved cultivars are especially good. They are slower to become established but less invasive.

PS: Not hardy in the Edmonton area.

Helianthemum spp

(rock rose, sun rose)

A Mediterranean native, *Helianthemum* produces 6-to-12-inch-deep mounded mats of wiry branches that bear flat, roselike, ephemeral flowers about ⅓ inch across, over a long period in summer. The branches root as they spread. The plant needs full sun and limy or neutral soil with excellent drainage – sandy, gravelly and stony ground suits *Helianthemum* well. It does not transplant easily and is best if pot-grown while young. Plant 12 to 15 inches apart. Propagate by seeds or cuttings.

TC: *Helianthemum nummularium* should be cut back lightly in spring to encourage new growth that will carry the summer flowers of pink, red or yellow. Given full sun and reliable winter snow cover, the plant will survive quite low temperatures (minus 40 degrees F in Ottawa).

BJ: *Helianthemum alpestre* is the species usually associated with ground covers. I have not seen it in Newfoundland and very much doubt that it would be of any use here. However, *H. nummularium* forms a pleasant small shrub for the rock garden when grown in full sun and a deep, rather lean soil. It requires winter protection and careful attention in order to survive and look its best here.

AP: The grey foliage forms are especially good.

GS: Not very commonly seen in Vancouver, but thrives on sunny slopes. Should be more widely grown.

PS: The large-flowered *Helianthemum*

2:1

varieties are not reliably hardy in the Edmonton area.

Hemerocallis spp

(day lily)

1:3

Modern hybrid day lilies are a far cry from the old orange form often seen naturalized along roadsides. Now, day lilies come in a range of heights, from 15 inches to about 4 feet, with wide trumpet lily blooms in all shades from creamy white, yellow and orange through pink and red to purple, flowering over a long season from late June to early September. All have tall, grassy, arching leaves. They will grow in full sun or in shade (but do not flower as well in shade) and in most soils, sandy or clay, although they do best in a good soil containing plenty of organic matter. Give them ample water, especially during the growing season. The fleshy roots grow near the surface, so avoid deep or careless cultivation. Plant about 2 feet apart, and weed between the plants for the first year or so. To maintain flower performance, pull up the plants, divide them and replant in replenished soil every four or five years.

BJ: Could be useful as a tall ground cover for small areas, in full sun.

AP: The old forms are best for rough-bank ground covers.

GS: One of the best tall, grasslike ground covers with lovely flowers, especially where the summers are hot and sunny. Not as good on the Pacific coast, as the flowers don't open well when we have cool, wet days. Thousands of cultivars are now available, including some smaller ones.

PS: Generally speaking, the older hybrids are much hardier than the modern pastel ones. The clumps are easily invaded by quack grass.

Herniaria glabra

(rupturewort)

1:1

Rupturewort spreads by rooting stems to form a glossy, dark green carpet a few inches high. It has small, inconspicuous green flowers. An evergreen perennial in warm areas, it may have to be treated as an annual where winters are harsh. Place plants 6 to 8 inches apart.

BJ: These plants form dense mats of minute greenish bronze leaves and are 63 suitable as ground cover with dwarf bulbs or for placement between the crevices of rock walkways. They can be propagated by seed or by division. They seem to do best in sun but do not like to be baked. Give them good drainage.

Hosta spp

(hosta, plantain lily, funkia)

Grown mainly for their attractive, broad, deciduous foliage (which may be green, bluish, gold or variegated), hostas are valuable ground covers for shady areas. Some of them have interesting spikes of lilylike white, purple or mauve

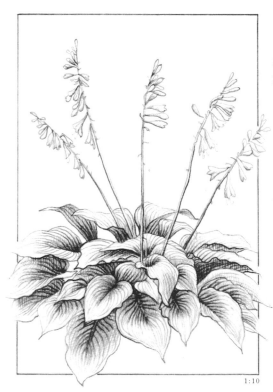

1:10

flowers. The plants require good, organically rich soil and must be kept well watered, especially in dry weather. Grow them (slowly) from seed started indoors or from divisions planted 2 feet apart.

TC: One of the best of all ground covers for shady areas. There are several hun-

dred named forms, but most are available only from specialist nurseries. The species *Hosta plantaginea* is fall-flowering and very fragrant. The main drawback of hostas is that they are among the favourite foods of slugs. By the end of the season, the leaves may be riddled with holes.

BJ: Hostas have great potential as ground covers for small areas in shade. They are not used as much as they could be in Newfoundland, and a considerable effort could be expended to find out which of the many species and hybrids are suitable here.

AP: An invaluable and now vast group. All take shade, but *Hosta plantaginea* will flower only in sun.

GS: Among the best clumped perennials for shaded locations, where the bold foliage and white-to-purple flowers are effective accents. Slug damage to the foliage is a problem on the Pacific coast.

PS: Good, solid ground cover plants for moist to normal soil. Sometimes the emerging foliage is caught by a late frost but will regrow. Plant away from the early-morning sun.

Hypericum spp

(St. John's wort)

This is a big genus of mainly shrubby, medicinal herbs with glossy green leaves and roselike yellow flowers. The best ground cover forms, with flowers as large as 3½ inches across, are hardy only in the mildest parts of the country. Most species tolerate sun or shade, are easy to cultivate and can be propagated by seeds, division and greenwood cuttings.

TC: These plants do well in sandy soils and full sun where their bright yellow flowers appear in midsummer. *Hypericum buckleyi, H. calycinum* and *H. moseranum* are three of the best.

BJ: Hypericums are now receiving a bit of interest in the St. John's area. *Hypericum olympicum* does very well in full sun and deep, well-drained soil, but this variety requires a reliable snow cover.

AP: Best for ground cover are *Hypericum calycinum* and *H. olympicum*. *H. calycinum* has the biggest flowers of the genus, is a foot high and runs vigorously. Give it full sun. It covers dry banks well. *H. olympicum* is less robust but makes wide, low clumps of greyish leaves and yellow flowers. Give it full sun and good drainage.

1:3

GS: *Hypericum calycinum* is one of the most common ground covers in southwestern British Columbia. Bright green, opposite pairs of leaves on arching stems and large five-petalled flowers in summer are showy. It thrives in full sun or light shade; it covers quickly and will exclude most weeds once established. Looks best if sheared back to the ground in early spring before new growth begins. Requires little care.

PS: Not hardy in the Edmonton area.

Iberis sempervirens

(evergreen candytuft)

As the genus name suggests, this member of the mustard family, Cruciferae, is a native of the western Mediterranean. The dwarf evergreen shrub forms a wide, 6-to-12-inch-deep mat of dark green narrow leaves. Heads of pure white flowers appear in spring and occasionally throughout the summer. In time, each plant will grow about 18 inches across, so start them 12 to 15 inches apart. Propagate from seeds or cuttings taken soon after flowering, and plant in good, well-drained soil in full sun. The abundant flower heads must be sheared off immediately after fading.

TC: It is very hardy and does not seem to winterburn.

BJ: Grows well in the St. John's area, forming a pleasant, medium-height ground cover. The cultivars 'Little Gem' and 'Snowflake' are particularly floriferous but are inclined to suffer some spring wind-

1:1

burn, so shelter them from prevailing spring winds. A reliable snow cover is also beneficial.

GS: Good for small areas and attractive on sunny walls or rock crevices. Usually grown mixed with *Aubrieta*, *Arabis* and *Aurinia*. Should be cut back from time to time to keep it bushy.

PS: Not reliably hardy as a ground cover in the Edmonton area.

Iris spp

(iris)

The tall, bearded types of iris do not make good ground covers, as their open form of growth allows too many weeds to become established, but the dwarf bearded types, which flower in spring, are closer-growing and will crowd out weeds. The crested iris (*Iris cristata*) produces thin leaves and purple flowers in late spring or early summer and forms thick mats of rhizomes on the soil surface. Divide the rhizomes to propagate.

1:2

TC: The native *Iris cristata* is useful as a ground cover in light shade. The rhizomes on this are thin and wiry, and it is easy to maintain.

AP: A huge genus. Few make much ground cover effect, although *Iris cristata* and *I. florentina* are possibilities.

GS: The low-growing *Iris cristata* is sometimes used as a ground cover in sun or in light shade. It is very attractive in spring when the purple flowers are out.

PS: Dwarf bearded German irises make a good, colourful ground cover for warm, south-facing areas. They need to be divided every three years, or the plants will decrease in size and in number of flowers.

Juniperus spp

(juniper)

Evergreen, easily cared for and attractive all year, the prostrate forms of juniper are among the most popular ground covers, especially in foundation plantings near houses. There are many species and cultivars with various growth characteristics and colours. Plant junipers about 3 feet apart—depending on the ultimate spread—in good, well-drained, organically rich soil. Once established, junipers seem to do best in hot dry places in full sun and will tolerate no more than half shade. In the fall, they can be readily, though somewhat slowly, propagated from tip cuttings of hardened new growth.

TC: Almost all of the prostrate forms of juniper can be used as ground covers. Many will root where they touch the soil, and because they cast dark shade, junipers control all but the most rampant of weeds. The chief objection to their use is their cost.

BJ: Many junipers have potential as ground cover plants, but not all will thrive in Newfoundland. *Juniperus communis* and *J. horizontalis* are native species, so varieties of these will do well. *J. horizontalis* forms a particularly dense, prostrate mat and is available in a variety of interesting shades. Judicious collecting of cuttings from wild shrubs is a cheap but somewhat slow means of acquiring suitable plants.

AP: The genus includes many invaluable coniferous ground covers with green, grey and bluish forms. Some, such as 'Bar Harbor,' are prostrate, and others are much taller.

GS: Cannot tolerate wet conditions. Several of the low-growing species are raised here on the West Coast in dry

1:2

places, including *Juniperus horizontalis, J. conferta* and *J. communis* varieties. Still, weather conditions in Vancouver are not well-suited to the sun-loving junipers.

PS: *Juniperus horizontalis,* in its many varieties, is the most outstanding juniper for use as a ground cover. All of its varieties form large mats of tight green foliage that are attractive all year. The best cultivars are 'Prince of Wales' (deep green) and 'Dunvegan Blue' (blue-green). Other good cultivars are 'Bar Harbor,' 'Blue Chip,' 'Green Acres,' 'Hughes' and 'Wiltonii.' *J. chinensis* tends to suffer winter damage here in Edmonton, while *J. communis* 'Crowfoot,' which forms a feathery, dense 18-inch mat, is a very good variety that turns bronze-green in fall; *J. sabina* 'Scandia' is shorter (about 10 inches high) and a good solid ground cover.

Lamium spp

(dead-nettle)

Many dead-nettles are weeds, but a couple of the perennial species are useful as ground covers and are easy to grow in full sun or light shade. They have opposite toothed leaves often blotched yellow or white along the midrib and will form a loose mat about 8 inches high in sun or shade. Propagate them by seed or by division, and plant 12 inches apart.

TC: The yellow archangel (*Lamium galeobdolon* 'Florentium') is a slow-growing plant good for small areas, while the spotted dead-nettle (*L. maculatum*), which has purple flowers and leaves with white stripes and blotches, is more vigorous.

AP: *Lamium maculatum*, especially in its silver form ('Beacon Silver'), is valuable in full shade, where it produces small heads of pink or white flowers. *L. galeobdolon* (also called *Lamiastrum galeobdolon*), with yellow flower spikes, is much more robust and can become a pest in small gardens. It thrives under trees.

GS: Attractive in spring when the new growth and flowers are best; it tends to look scrubby in midsummer and better again in autumn. Several variegated forms are usually cultivated, such as 'Beacon Silver,' with silvery leaves and purple-mauve flowers.

1:2

PS: *Lamium maculatum* and its cultivars 'Album' (white flowers), 'Beacon Silver' and 'Chequers' (both with variegated leaves) form a solid carpet. In this climate, it is a good idea to keep a few young plants for replacement, as *Lamium* can sometimes die back in a severe win- 67 ter. *L. galeobdolon* is not a good ground cover in the Edmonton area.

Linnaea borealis

(twinflower)

Twinflower is a trailing, evergreen, somewhat woody vine that thrives in moist, peaty or leafy soil, forming a mat several inches deep. The roundish leaves are an inch long, and the bell-shaped flowers are just ⅓ inch across in summer. Plant about 12 inches apart. This is difficult to grow unless conditions are just right for it.

1:2

BJ: This beautiful little native ground cover prefers light shade but can grow in full sun, provided ground moisture and humidity are maintained. It loves to associate with an old log or stump. Increase by division of the rooted sections of the trailing stems; establish divisions in moist, humus-rich, acidic soil in shade. If necessary, top-dress with a mixture of very fine peat and leaf mould. The tiny pink flowers

have a delicate scent, so plant them in a windless area where they can be enjoyed.

Lobularia maritima

(annual alyssum)

This common bedding plant is an annual that blooms constantly from summer to fall. Less than a foot tall, it has narrow, greyish leaves and flowers that range from white to pink and from rose to purple. It can be used to fill areas between slower-growing perennial ground covers.

TC: In most areas, this annual will reseed itself year after year. It is easy to grow from seed sown directly (scattered over the area) or started indoors in late April and transplanted to 12 inches apart. Weeding by hand will be required in seeded areas to give the flowers a chance. The white forms seem to establish themselves slightly better than the mauve ones.

1:2

BJ: The semihardy annual alyssums make colourful and highly scented ground covers for rich soil in full sun. Use them as trim along the edge of a formal bed in good-sized clumps, where their delightful scent can fill the air.

Lonicera spp

(honeysuckle)

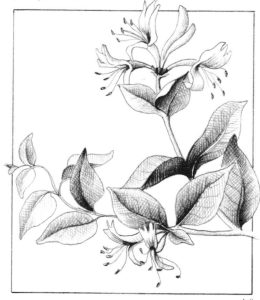

1:2

The best-known honeysuckles are flowering vines with fragrant, white summer flowers that fade to yellow. A number of these will form carpets several feet deep if denied something to climb. Plant them in sun or light shade in moist but well-drained soil that contains plenty of organic matter. Pin down the trailing shoots at a node to encourage rooting. Propagate by division or cuttings.

TC: The hardy 'Dropmore Scarlet' never makes a good thick ground cover, but the more tender Hall's honeysuckle (*Lonicera japonica halliana*) has become a pest in some areas of the United States. It roots wherever it touches the soil and is hard to contain. It will climb and choke to death any tree or shrub it encounters.

BJ: Two climbing honeysuckles, *Lonicera periclymenum* and *L. sempervirens*, grow and flower very well in the St. John's area. Both can be allowed to trail on the ground, but it sometimes requires considerable effort to keep them clear of weeds. They are susceptible to a small caterpillar that eats young shoots and can destroy the flowers if not controlled.

AP: Honeysuckles are best used as climbers as God intended, but *Lonicera japonica aureo-reticulata*, with gold-netted leaves, succeeds as a ground cover. *L. japonica halliana* is the same and flowers well. It becomes a weed in warm climates.

GS: Mostly grown as a climbing vine here on the Pacific coast, *Lonicera japonica* has very fragrant summer flowers and can be used as a scrambling ground cover. It may become weedy and invasive.

PS: Not grown here in Edmonton as a ground cover.

Lotus corniculatus

(bird's-foot trefoil)

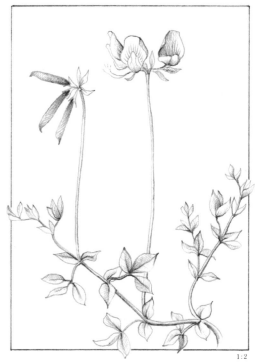

1:2

A member of the pea family Leguminosae and therefore capable of fixing its own nitrogen, this 18-inch or smaller 69 vetch, with attractive yellow flowers in late summer, is grown as a forage crop and is often found on the edges of fields and along roadsides. Propagate by seeds or by careful division in spring, and plant in any well-drained soil in sun.

TC: A charming weed that takes well to cultivation. There is a double form, but it is not nearly as good a ground cover in the Ottawa area.

BJ: An alien species that has established itself in the wild. I have never seen it used deliberately as a ground cover in Newfoundland, but it may have limited potential for some sites.

AP: Not much to recommend it as a ground cover, but it is best on poor, limy soil.

GS: Most often seen mixed with *Coronilla* and grasses on rough banks. The yellow flowers are showy, but it is not used much on the West Coast except in highway plantings.

PS: A good but short-lived thick ground cover. There is a very attractive double-flowered form.

1:1

Lysimachia nummularia

(moneywort, creeping Jennie)

A very easy-to-grow, pretty little plant whose completely flat, trailing branches have green or golden leaves and bright yellow flowers at ground level in summer. It does best on wettish, heavy soils but is often found growing in the crevices of walls. It will tolerate full shade. Moneywort is easily propagated from self-rooted stems. Encourage this plant to thicken by periodically pinching off the tips of its trailing stems.

TC: A good plant for many areas, even though it is inclined to be invasive. There is also a form with yellow leaves that will grow equally well in sun or shade.

BJ: Creeping Jennie grows well in the St. John's area and will make a good ground cover in light shade. If situated near less robust plants, take care that

its aggressiveness does not swamp everything around it.

GS: Does very well in southwestern British Columbia, but it is not very often seen here.

PS: Not grown here in the Edmonton area.

Mahonia spp

(Oregon grape, creeping mahonia)

These native evergreen shrubs, which can be less than a foot to several feet tall, depending on species and climate, have shiny green or purple-flushed leaves and bright yellow spring flowers followed by edible fruit that is attractive to birds. Propagate by seed, suckers, layering or cuttings, and plant in moist soil in light shade. Protect the mahonias from strong wind and hot sun.

TC: *Mahonia aquifolium* suffers winter damage above the snowline in climatic zone 5 or colder but soon puts out new foliage in the spring to hide the damage. Clusters of bright yellow flowers in spring are followed by black, edible, grapelike clusters of fruit. Plant about 3 feet apart. Creeping mahonia (*M. repens*) is lower-

1:4

tiny leaves and blue or purplish lobelialike flowers in spring. It spreads by rooting along its trailing stems. Propagate by division or seed, and plant 6 inches apart in moist soil in sun or shade.

TC: It is of borderline hardiness here in Ottawa, where a colder-than-average winter killed the plants; however, it is quite aggressive and should make a fine ground cover where it is hardy. During the four or five years it survived, it soon recovered from winter injury.

BJ: I cannot recall ever seeing it here in the St. John's area.

1:1

growing but spreads slowly by underground runners. Eventually, it makes a better ground cover.

BJ: Occasionally grown in the St. John's area for foundation planting or in a shrub border. I have never seen it used here as a ground cover. *Mahonia* requires a sheltered area to do well.

AP: The lower-growing forms are best for ground covers, but all are invaluable.

GS: Too tall to be used as a ground cover in southwestern British Columbia, but sometimes used as a mass shrub planting. Mahonias are slow to become established but good once settled.

PS: *Mahonia aquifolium* is not hardy here in Edmonton, but *M. repens* will form a light ground cover in partial shade on well-drained soil. It grows 8 inches tall.

Mazus reptans

(creeping mazus)

A very prostrate (only 1 or 2 inches high), bright green, creeping plant with

AP: It is good between paving stones but cannot take much wear.

GS: Attractive, but it tends to become invasive and can be a problem if it creeps into grassy areas. Not often grown.

PS: Not hardy in the Edmonton area.

Nepeta spp

(catmint, catnip)

Although there are both annual and perennial species of *Nepeta*, including the herb catnip, the best species for ground covers are the clump-forming or creeping perennials. Most have greyish foliage and clouds of lavender-blue flowers in spring. Cut back after flowering for a second

71

flush. The rampant gill-over-the-ground, or ground ivy (*N. hederacea* or *Glechoma hederacea*), is fragrant, floral and attractive, but it spreads so rapidly and vigorously by rooting from its trailing stems that it can easily invade lawns. Grow *Nepeta* from seed or by division.

1:2

TC: Many of the catmints are weedy. If you don't object to visits by the neighbourhood cats, catnip itself (*Nepeta cataria*) can be used, but the best species for ground cover is Faassens catmint (*N. faassenii*), which grows about 1 foot tall and has silvery leaves and pale blue flowers. Plants spread quite rapidly and should be planted about 18 inches apart in full sun. Propagate by division.

BJ: If not watched carefully, the nepetas will quickly make a nuisance of themselves by trying to take over choicer areas of the garden. Ground ivy has naturalized in Newfoundland and should be used as a ground cover only after careful thought.

AP: *Nepeta faassenii* is the best form, at 18 inches. *N. gigantea* is twice the size.

GS: *Nepeta faassenii* is the most common type grown on the West Coast. The grey-green foliage is fragrant, and the plants are very attractive when they bloom in spring. Good in small areas in full sun. The foliage is attractive to cats, which eat, dig and roll in the plants.

PS: *Nepeta hederacea* can be used in shade but is very invasive.

Pachysandra terminalis

(Japanese spurge)

A constant and dependable foot-tall evergreen, this is the cover most people use in shady places. It is hardy, tolerant of drought and quick to fill in by underground runners. Propagate by cuttings, and plant 1 foot apart in good, moist, slightly acidic soil.

TC: Despite all its attributes, I remain unenthusiastic about *Pachysandra terminalis* and seldom use it.

BJ: In theory, this plant should grow well in the St. John's area, but the plants do not seem to survive longer than three or four years.

AP: White flower spikes in summer add little interest, but the slow-growing variegated form is worth the search. The bark of *Pachysandra* shrubs is quite appealing to mice and voles, so some protection may be warranted.

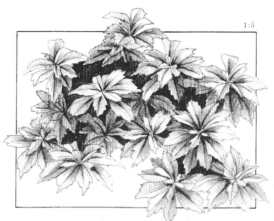

1:5

GS: One of the best evergreen ground covers and an old standby for shade, but it burns in full sun. It is slow to establish but is good once started. The flowers are insignificant. The variegated (white-edged) forms are less vigorous but attractive.

PS: In the Edmonton area, it does not form the dense cover it does in milder climates.

Paxistima canbyi

(pachistima, Canby's paxistima)

One of the most commonly grown ground covers, this foot-high evergreen shrub resembles boxwood, with tiny dark green leaves. It roots from spreading branches, and although it will eventually make a solid mat of intertwining stems that choke out all weeds, it can take a long time to reach this stage, especially in alkaline soils. It prefers a slightly acidic soil, where it does well both in sun and shade. *Paxistima* grows quite readily from cuttings. Plant 2 feet apart.

1:1

TC: This species is hardier than the myrtle pachistima (*Paxistima myrsinites*), its western counterpart.

BJ: Usually considered too difficult to acquire and too expensive to use as a ground cover in the St. John's area. If planted in good, rich organic soil in sun or light shade, however, it could spread sufficiently to form a medium-height cover for small choice areas. It requires reliable snow cover, and the site where it is growing should not be allowed to dry out. It makes an interesting specimen plant amongst small rhododendrons.

AP: A particularly dreary little evergreen, slow to grow and not worth waiting for anyway.

GS: A southern Appalachian native that should be planted more often than it is.

PS: Not recommended – grows poorly and is winterkilled readily here in Edmonton.

Phlox subulata

(moss phlox, moss pink)

A low, spreading phlox that forms wide, 4-to-6-inch-high mats of narrow, slightly prickly leaves and brilliant displays of white, pink, rose or mauve flowers in early summer. In rich, well-drained soil in full sun, the plants spread quite quickly, forming a dense mat that chokes out weeds. Shear lightly after flowering to promote new growth. Propagates easily by division or by cuttings in summer. Plant 12 to 18 inches apart.

TC: An almost perfect ground cover in full sun.

BJ: Has done well in Newfoundland for many years. Do not plant in soil that is too rich, or it will become leggy and will flower less.

AP: A good rock garden cover.

GS: Sometimes grown here in the Vancouver area, in rock walls or crevices, in full sun, with *Arabis* and the other wall plants. But it is not seen here as much as it is in hotter areas.

1:1

PS: Very colourful, and excellent in hot dry situations. It needs to be clipped back after flowering. Growing well at the botanic gardens in Edmonton are the cultivars 'Beauty of Rosdorf,' 'Nelsonii,' 'Scarlet Flame' and 'Vivid.' 'Rosette' has formed patches 3 feet across. Any variety is worth trying.

Pinus mugo mugo

(dwarf mugo pine)

A low, spreading evergreen shrub or small tree that produces solid, heavy clumps of typical pine foliage, dark and heavy in effect. It may grow 3 to 20 feet tall, depending on selection, soil and climate. Give it no more than half shade. Trim back hard after shoot growth if the shape and size are to be maintained.

TC: Too slow-growing to be effective.

GS: A shrubby plant that is sometimes used as a mass planting on large slopes or as a tall cover on berms, giving good, dark

green colour year-round. Easy in full sun on well-drained soil.

PS: Stands up well to extreme cold. A better ground cover variety is *Pinus mugo minimalis*, which is similar to *P. mugo mugo* but more dwarf.

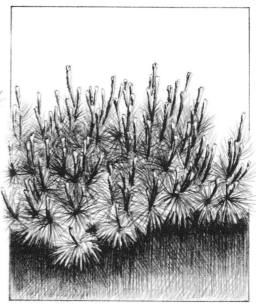

1:5

Polygonum spp

(fleece-flower, knotweed)

There are about 300 species in the genus *Polygonum*, whose name means "many knees" in honour of the swollen-jointed stems that suggest bamboo. The different species vary from a few inches to several feet tall and from weeds to valued ornamentals. Propagate by seed or by division.

TC: There are three perennial polygonums that can be considered ground covers. The Himalayan fleece-flower (*Polygonum affine*) is a dwarf plant often grown in rock gardens. It has pink flowers on 6-inch stems in early fall, followed by attractive brownish seeds. Reynoutria fleece-flower is taller (12 inches) and flowers in midsummer. Both spread slowly by runners. The third species is a most invasive weed and should be considered only when all else fails. Japanese knotweed or Japanese bamboo (*P. cuspidatum*) will grow to 8 feet tall and spreads wildly. It is most attractive when in flower but is not to be encouraged. There are also some dwarf forms that are equally invasive and will grow in sun or partial shade. An annual polygonum which has appeared in seed catalogues in recent years and which makes a good ground cover for small areas is *P. capitatum* 'Magic Carpet,' whose bronze leaves have a dark V mark. The small, pink globular flowers bloom for much of the summer. Grow it in full sun, as the dark foliage does not show up in the shade. It will self-seed.

BJ: The potential of these plants is yet to be fully understood in the St. John's area. Preliminary indications are that they are not as hardy as we may wish and that their survival may depend on a reliable and early snow cover. *Polygonum vaccinifolium* is a pleasant, deciduous ground cover suitable for planting beneath large rhododendrons. *P. bistorta* flowers well for us in full sun but is a more compact, less rampant spreader.

AP: *Polygonum cuspidatum* is a magnificent but lethal bamboolike plant best not brought into any small garden. *P. bistorta* could be a good ground cover for moist soils. It has spikes of pink flowers. *P. campanulatum* bears pink bells on 5-foot plants in autumn. *P. affine* has flat growth and pink flowers in summer and fall.

GS: *Polygonum affine* slowly forms dense mats of low green leaves that turn red or coppery in autumn. Tall spikes of pink flowers in midsummer to late autumn fade to dark pink. The plants look better if the spent flower stalks are sheared off. *P. vaccinifolium* produces wiry mats of small green leaves and masses of soft pink flowers in late summer and autumn. Both of these species are suitable but not often grown.

PS: *Polygonum bistorta* forms a dense matted cover to 8 inches high, spreads

1:3

slowly and is herbaceous. With small pink flowers on short spikes on foot-tall stems, it is more valuable for its foliage than for its flowers. Seems to adapt well to lean soil conditions.

Potentilla spp

(cinquefoil)

Best known for ornamental, long-blooming shrubs, the genus *Potentilla* also includes a number of low-growing species that are good as deciduous or semi-evergreen ground covers. All have attractive compound leaves and tolerate drought and hot sunny conditions. The small, wild-roselike flowers are usually yellow but sometimes white or red. Spring cinquefoil (*Potentilla verna*) produces a 3-to-6-inch-thick mat, while other types are somewhat larger, although all withstand clipping well. Propagate by seed or by division.

TC: Depending upon the area involved, there is a cinquefoil to suit every need. For small sites, use one of the rock garden types, such as *Potentilla verna verna* or the native three-toothed cinquefoil (*P. tri-*

1:1

dentata). In larger areas, the named perennial forms, such as 'Gibson's Scarlet' and 'Glory of Nancy,' will do well. For large spaces, the woody cinquefoil (*P. fruticosa*) in its many named forms will, with time, give a thick ground cover.

BJ: *Potentilla tridentata* is a little native flower that can thrive in some very poor soils and on rather dry sites; nevertheless, it should not be allowed to bake, so a little moist peat in the soil will help conserve some slight dampness. It has small white clustered flowers and leaves that turn a brilliant blood-red in fall. Easily propagated from cuttings or by division, it is one of the small ground covers suitable for underplanting with miniature bulbs.

AP: Look for *Potentilla anserina* with silver foliage and yellow flowers and *P. reptans* 'Pleniflora,' a double-flowered form of vigorous ground cover best kept confined. It will grow in poorly drained ground.

GS: Easy and good, but not usually strong enough to exclude weeds. Low forms of the shrubby *Potentilla fruticosa* are often used as taller ground covers and are easily adapted to a wide range of growing conditions and climates.

PS: All the cultivars of *Potentilla fruticosa*, deciduous shrubs up to 3 feet tall, do well in the Edmonton area. Their flowers vary from white to cream, deep yellow and orange. Recommended cultivars include 'Kathryn Dykes,' 'Primrose Beauty'

and 'Coronation Triumph.' 'Daydawn' produces pink flowers later in the season when it is cooler. 'Red Ace' and 'Tangerine' are likewise faded in hot weather and produce their best flowers in fall. *P. fruticosa minima* makes a slow-growing, low mound up to a foot high and has few flowers but dense foliage.

Rosa spp

(rose)

Most roses are shrubby ornamentals that have been grafted to nonsuckering rootstocks, but a few ramblers, if not grafted, will make prickly ground covers several feet tall, best suited to farms and to otherwise unusable hillsides. Most have single pink, white or scarlet flowers. Propagate by cuttings or by layering, and plant about 30 inches apart in a sunny, well-drained location.

1:1

TC: While roses make excellent hedges, the few that are good as ground covers take a long time to make a weed-free cover. The smooth rose (*Rosa blanda*) spreads underground and is useful for binding slopes. In warmer areas, the Japanese rose (*R. multiflora*) can be grown, but it has become a menace in parts of the United States. One of the new *R. rugosa* hybrids developed at the Central Experimental Farm in Ottawa, 'Charles Albanel,' is low-growing and was selected for its potential as a ground cover.

BJ: Aside from the two native species and a few very old shrub roses, this genus is too temperamental in St. John's.

AP: Many could be considered. Species good for ground covers include *Rosa wichuraiana, R. nitida* and *R. rugosa*. Look for the hybrid *R.* 'Max Graf.' Most gallicas on their own roots, such as 'Versicolor' or 'Officinalis,' are also suitable.

GS: Shrubby *Rosa rugosa* can be used to a limited degree as a tall cover for large plantings, if the plants are grown close together. Some of the lower-spreading roses, such as 'The Fairy,' have potential as ground covers and for cascading over garden walls.

PS: *Rosa rugosa* 'Mrs. Anthony Waterer' forms a wide, spreading, dense bush about 3 feet tall in the Edmonton area. Provided it is on its own roots, it spreads to form a large clump 5 feet across. It has double magenta flowers and good, crisp dark green foliage. *R. rugosa* 'Frau Dagmar Hartopp' is somewhat similar in growth but is shorter and has single pink flowers.

Sagina subulata

(Pearlwort, Irish-moss, Scotch moss)

Until the tiny white flowers appear, this evergreen species looks just like a moss. It forms a low tufted carpet 3 or 4 inches high and is similar to *Arenaria*, but with finer foliage. Plant it in rich, moist but well-drained soil in sun or in light shade. Propagate by division.

TC: Slow growing, but it seeds itself into cracks and crevices and is a suitable cover for rustic paths and similar small areas.

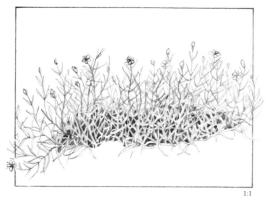

1:1

AP: Tiny leaves and minute flowers – good for paving cracks.

GS: Good for growing between paving stones. The golden forms are especially attractive. It tends to become invasive.

PS: Not hardy in Edmonton.

Saxifraga spp

(mossy saxifrage, rockfoil)

These alpine or encrusted saxifrages are herbaceous perennials with white, pink or purple flowers that bloom in late spring and early summer. Some, such as *Saxifraga oppositifolia*, are trailing ground-hugging plants; *S. hypnoides* forms cushions about 3 inches tall and 2 feet wide; and others have basal, clustered leaves and grow about 4 inches tall. Propagate by seed, by division or from cuttings taken shortly after flowering. Grow in average soil, in light shade.

BJ: The mossy saxifrages make good evergreen ground covers for small or medium-sized areas in the home garden. They require a cool, semishaded site in rich well-drained soil that never dries out. All suffer in hot, muggy weather and often die out at such times. The flowers are borne in great profusion on 4-to-8-inch stems. There are numerous named garden varieties that should be propagated from cuttings, not from seed. Cut the flower stalks off close to the leaves immediately after the flowers have faded.

PS: 'London pride' (*Saxifraga umbrosa*) 77

Some are first-rate ground covers, but others are so invasive that they should never be allowed into the garden. The best ones that are readily available are Kamtschatka stonecrop (*Sedum kamtschaticum*), which is evergreen, with yellow flowers in late summer; the two-row stonecrop (*S. spurium*), in various named forms, such as 'Dragon's Blood'; and in areas slightly warmer than Ottawa, the 'Cape Blanco' sedum. All three are mat-forming, but 'Cape Blanco' (sometimes called 'Capa Blanca') grows slowly and is best for small areas. Avoid the goldmoss stonecrop (*S. acre*), which will spread to all parts of the garden.

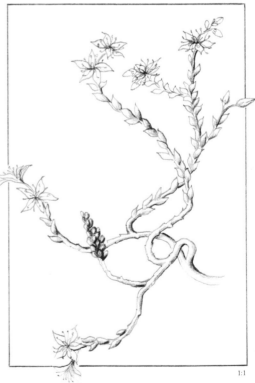

is a rosette-forming *Saxifraga* with yellow spotted leaves, and it forms solid stands quickly. It is commonly grown in the Edmonton area in sun or light shade. Soft pink flowers appear in spring.

Sedum spp

(stonecrop)

The ground-covering species of these fleshy-leaved succulent plants have a trailing habit and root at the stem joints. They are easy to grow, even in thin poor soil, and tolerate sun and shade. Propagate by seeds or by division, or press cuttings into the ground. These will generally root without difficulty. Trim off the flower heads after blooming, and lightly top-dress annually with a mixture of sand, soil and leaf mould.

TC: Treat stonecrops with caution.

BJ: This is a very large genus with many beautiful species but also some that are decidedly ugly. *Sedum spurium* and *S. kamtschaticum* show good potential as ground covers, while *S. acre* and *S. album* are useful for small areas.

AP: *Sedum acre* and *S. anglicum*, with yellow and pinkish flowers respectively, are suitable for very dry spots such as gravel edges. On a larger scale, the *S. maximum* or *S. spectabile* types could be tried. They have fine summer foliage and late-summer flowers. Consider also *S. spurium* 'Rose Carpet'; *S. sarmentosum*; *S. kamtschaticum* and *S. baileyi*.

GS: The low-growing species are good for hot, sunny locations, but they do not tolerate shade, wet soils or foot traffic, as they are brittle and break easily. Not seen as much on the West Coast, except in rock walls and very sunny places.

PS: Good ground cover for warm well-drained soils, especially in full sun. The following have done well in Edmonton: *Sedum ewersii, S. hybridum, S. integrifolia, S. kamtschaticum* and *S. spurium*. *S. spectabile* and its varieties normally bloom too late and are frequently frost-damaged.

Sempervivum spp

(hen and chickens, houseleek)

Another genus of fleshy, succulent plants. The relatively large, ground-hugging mother rosettes produce smaller offsets that, in turn, grow and produce offsets of their own – an attractive habit that gives the plant its common name. Sempervivums vary in colour from green to bronze. Plant individual rosettes about 6 inches apart in sandy soil, and be prepared to weed by hand for the first couple of years. Replace dead rosettes with fresh young offsets broken from the outside of older plants; offsets root extremely easily.

TC: One of my favourite ground covers for small places. The variation among the numerous species and named forms is fantastic, and a mass planting of a number of different hybrids can be a real showpiece. Because of their nature, sempervivums are not plants to use where there is any chance of their being walked over. Place stepping stones throughout the planting so you can remove dead rosettes

1:1

once flowering starts.

BJ: An interesting texture diversity can be arranged by the careful choice of species and varieties.

AP: Only a weak cover, but useful above alpine bulbs.

GS: Good to mix with sedums. The round rosettes or leaves are a nice contrast to the smaller leaves of the sedums.

PS: Excellent ground cover for hot, dry situations. It is extremely hardy and will spread quite rapidly by rosettes. In full sun, the older rosettes produce yellow or pinkish flowers, and toward fall, the rosettes curl inward as a protection against extreme cold. Some 40 varieties grow at the botanical garden here in Edmonton.

Stachys olympica, S. lanata

(lamb's ear)

A very distinctive plant with felted, silver leaves and fuzzy spikes of tiny pink flowers, lamb's ear produces an unusual and attractive ground cover in a sunny place. It grows about 18 inches high, and plants placed 12 inches apart will soon fill

79

in. Full sun allows them to remain their greyest and most compact, although they will take dry shade under deciduous trees. Each plant eventually forms a clump about 3 feet wide. Lamb's ear is not too fussy about soil quality, provided drainage is adequate. Propagate by division.

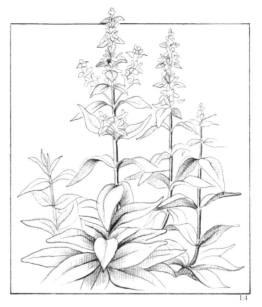

1:4

TC: The flowers are not showy and are best removed when young.

BJ: In St. John's, it needs to be planted on very well-drained soil because the felt-like leaves hate moisture, especially periods of wet snow. The form 'Silver Carpet,' which seldom flowers, is reputed to be especially suitable as a ground cover.

AP: The best grey ground cover. 'Silver Carpet' is a nonflowering form — a pity, really.

GS: Very pleasing and easy.

PS: Not reliably hardy in the Edmonton area; it frequently suffers winterkill.

Symphoricarpos chenultii 'Hancock'

(Hancock's coralberry)

A prostrate form of a native North American snowberry that produces decorative white fruit, which is retained long into winter. The plant grows about 3 feet tall and spreads by suckers. Plant in either sun or in shade, on any well-drained soil. It is hardy to Canadian climatic zone 5. Propagate by division.

TC: This is a dwarf spreading form of the common coralberry. It does not flower and fruit as profusely as the more upright forms but is widely used as a ground cover, especially in Europe. This variety originated at Woodland Nursery, Mississauga, Ontario.

Thymus spp

(thyme)

There are several species of thyme, many named forms selected from these, and there is considerable taxonomic debate surrounding the entire genus. However, there is little confusion regarding these plants as ground covers. Nearly all form undulating mounds of pleasantly scented foliage a few inches deep, bear white-to-purple spring flowers and are very useful between stones on a patio or path; all will stand up to some foot traffic without damage, and all require full sun and soil that is not too rich. They are very easily grown from seed (which is tiny) or propagated by cuttings or division. Plant them 6 inches apart in well-drained soil, in sun or in light shade. All are useful as kitchen herbs as well.

TC: Look for caraway thyme (*Thymus herba-barona*); mother-of-thyme (*T. serpyllum*), with its distinctive fragrance; lemon thyme (*T.s. citriodorus*), which is lemon-scented; and woolly thyme (*T. lanuginosus*), with grey foliage.

BJ: These plants make ideal ground covers for the edges of footpaths or between flagstones of steps and walkways. In the St. John's area, try *Thymus serpyllum angustifolium*, with purple flowers or *T.s.* 'Montanus albus,' with white flowers. For greyish foliage and pale purple flowers, use *T. lanuginosus*. All are very aromatic and ideal for areas visited by blind persons.

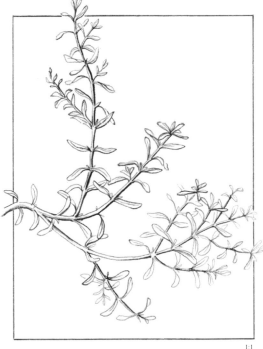

1:1

AP: *Thymus serpyllum* and *T. lanuginosus* make excellent, completely flat covers with purple, white or pink flowers; good between paving stones.

GS: Low-growing species, especially the woolly thymes, are among the best ground covers for sunny locations. Once established, they will crowd out weeds.

PS: *Thymus serpyllum* and its varieties are excellent ground covers. Older patches tend to die in the centre, so the plants need to be lifted and replanted every three years.

Trifolium repens

(white clover)

A low creeping perennial with the typical three-part leaves of the genus and sweetly scented white flowers, this clover forms a loose cover several inches high. Because it is a nitrogen fixer, it can establish itself on very impoverished soil but will take time to do so. The flowers attract bees—an advantage or a detriment according to one's point of view. White clover is easily grown from seeds broadcast in spring on moist soil and then lightly covered.

TC: In large or naturalistic gardens, white clover could find a home. I feel that it is a bit too coarse for use in the small garden.

BJ: A valuable ground cover plant in the St. John's area, especially in natural or seminatural sites.

1:1

81

AP: Seldom grown as a pure stand, but when it is used in high proportion in a grass sward, it offers a restricted mowing regime and bee-pleasing white flowers. It is also useful on steep banks.

GS: Good to mix with grasses as a lawn, but it is considered a weed by the lawn purists.

PS: Has not been tried as a ground cover in the Edmonton area.

Vancouveria planipetala

(American barrenwort, inside-out flower)

1:3

This western native with elegant, light green foliage and small white flowers grows to 1½ feet tall in summer and dies back to the ground in winter. A woodland plant, it needs moist, acidic, organic soil in shade and so combines well with *Epimedium* and ferns where it is hardy. It spreads by rhizomes. Propagate by division, and plant 12 inches apart.

TC: Not hardy in the Ottawa region.

BJ: I have not seen this plant in St. John's.

AP: Like a small, delicate *Epimedium*; it offers a similar effect in shade.

GS: A good evergreen ground cover for shade, but invasive in the Vancouver area.

PS: Not grown in Edmonton.

Vinca minor

(lesser periwinkle)

A delightful, prostrate, evergreen ground cover that produces a mat of shiny, usually dark green leaves about 6 inches deep. The trailing stems root as they spread. It is very easily propagated from cuttings poked into a mixture of peat and sand or simply into a damp, shady area of the garden. Flowers are usually lilac-blue, but there are also white- and purple-flowered forms and some with variegated foliage. A sandy, moist but well-drained loam is ideal, but these plants will grow in any reasonably good, moisture-retentive soil in sun or in light shade.

TC: A very useful ground cover for shade. It grows slowly and seldom makes

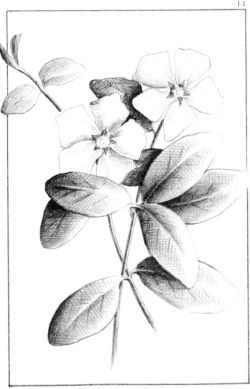

1:1

a completely weedfree mat, but despite these faults, I would rather have *Vinca* than *Pachysandra*. When it is grown beneath shrubs, the blue flowers brighten the landscape. There are also forms with pink or white flowers and with variegated leaves, but these are less vigorous.

BJ: Does well in both sun and partial shade in the St. John's area.

AP: *Vinca major* is less frost-hardy, but *V. major* 'Elegantissima' succeeds well with me in Hamilton and is a lovely plant.

GS: One of the best and most widely grown ground covers for shade; commonly naturalized around the Vancouver area. *Vinca major* – taller, less evergreen and with larger leaves and flowers than *V. minor* – is fairly commonly grown here.

PS: Not hardy in Edmonton.

Viola spp

(violet)

The named forms of violet are cool-weather plants that thrive in spring and fall, when they produce their heart-shaped leaves and colourful blooms in abundance. A few species are useful as low ground covers. They flourish in good soil with ample moisture in light shade, and they are best treated as biennials, although many will self-seed and naturalize in the areas they favour. Propagate by seed or by division.

TC: There are a few native violets that can be naturalized and that are either perennial or will self-seed. They often grow naturally along the edges of woods among grasses, so they may not take kindly to a well-manicured, weedfree garden.

AP: I cannot really sort out species without working on them when they are in growth and flower in spring, but some, such as *Viola labratorica* with purple leaves, *V. papilionacea* and *V. striata* with white and blue flowers, offer much scope as ground covers.

GS: *Viola odorata* and *V. sororia* are

1:1

good for a wide range of climates and are tolerant of nearly full sun to fairly dark shade. They are very easy to grow, although slugs are a problem in Vancouver.

PS: No perennial species is recommended as a ground cover. For a temporary cover, *Viola tricolor* is quite useful and floriferous, but it can become weedy.

Waldsteinia ternata

(barren strawberry)

Like *Duchesnea indica*, this ground cover has attractive, glossy strawberry foliage, inedible red fruit and yellow, potentilla-like flowers. In sun or shade, its running habit builds up a solid cover 4 to 10 inches deep. Plant 12 inches apart in light, humus-rich soil, and propagate by seed or by division.

TC: There is a native barren strawberry, but *Waldsteinia* comes from Siberia and Japan. The plant is well-behaved, needs full sun and will withstand some traffic.

BJ: This plant thrives in Newfoundland. 83

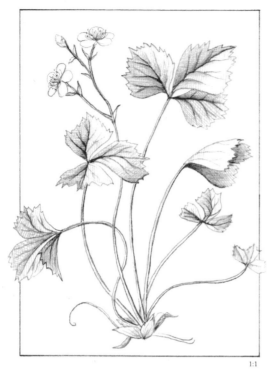

1:1

GS: A good strawberrylike plant for filtered shade. It grows well around Vancouver but is rarely seen.

PS: Not yet tried in Edmonton.

The Botanical Garden Curators List Their Favourite Ground Cover Plants For:

Shade

Aegopodium podagraria (BJ)
Ajuga reptans (BJ, GS)
Asarum spp (AP)
Asperula odorata (TC, AP)
Calluna vulgaris (TC)
Convallaria majalis (TC, BJ, PS)
Cornus canadensis (BJ)
Erica carnea (TC)
Gaultheria procumbens (BJ)
Hedera helix (AP, GS)
Hosta spp (TC, BJ)
Mahonia aquifolium (TC)
Nepeta spp (PS)

Pachysandra terminalis (TC, GS)
Vinca minor (TC, GS)

Steep Slopes

Achillea tomentosa (PS)
Aegopodium podagraria (TC: in rough areas where it cannot spread; AP, PS)
Ajuga reptans (TC)
Arctostaphylos uva-ursi (TC: if dry and sandy)
Cerastium tomentosum (PS)
Cotoneaster spp (BJ, GS)
Genista pilosa (BJ)
Hedera helix (BJ, AP, GS)
Hemerocallis spp (TC)
Hypericum calycinum (AP)
Juniperus horizontalis (TC: if the area is not too large; BJ, GS)
Lotus corniculatus (GS)
Ostrich Fern (TC)
Rosa spp (TC)
Salix spp (BJ)
Sempervivum spp (PS)

Very Cold Winters

(GS: not applicable here; PS: any plant I have described above)
Aegopodium podagraria (TC)
Arctostaphylos uva-ursi (BJ)
Cerastium tomentosum (TC)
Cornus canadensis (BJ)
Dianthus spp (TC)
Ferns (TC, BJ)
Juniperus communis (BJ)
Phlox subulata (TC)
Thymus spp (TC)

Winter Colour

Ajuga reptans (TC)
Arctostaphylos uva-ursi (AP)
Calluna vulgaris (GS: foliage)
Cornus sericea (TC)
Cotoneaster spp (TC, GS: berries)
Cotoneaster adpressa praecox (BJ)
Epimedium spp (AP)
Erica carnea (BJ, GS)

84

Euonymus fortunei (TC, AP)
Juniperus spp (TC)
Mahonia aquifolium (TC: in warmer
   locations)
Sempervivum spp (TC)

Dry Areas

Alyssum saxatile see *Aurina saxatile* (AP)
Antennaria dioica (TC)
Arabis caucasica (AP)
Arctostaphylos uva-ursi (TC)
Artemisia spp (PS)
Cerastium tomentosum (BJ)
Cytisus and *Genista* (TC)
Juniperus spp (GS, PS)
Opuntia spp (PS)
Sedum spp (TC, GS, PS)
Sempervivum spp (PS)
Thymus spp (TC)
Waldsteinia ternata (BJ)

Wet Areas

Astilbe chinensis (TC)
Convallaria majalis (AP)
Cornus sericea (TC)
Epimedium spp (TC)
Hemerocallis spp (PS)
Hosta spp (PS)
Iris spp (PS)
Lysimachia nummularia (TC, BJ)
Onoclea sensibilis see Ferns (AP)

Moderate Traffic Areas
(use lawn or paving for heavier traffic)

Aegopodium podagraria (TC)
Ajuga reptans (TC)
Antennaria dioica (TC)
Anthemis nobilis (TC)
Cerastium tomentosum (TC)
Duchesnea indica (TC: this one is tough)
Lotus corniculatus (TC)
Lysimachia nummularia (TC)
Phlox subulata (TC)
Sagina subulata (PS)
Thymus spp (TC, PS)
Trifolium repens (TC)

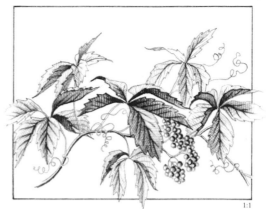

1:1

Climatic Zones

The climatic zone maps on the following
pages indicate general temperature
trends throughout Canada and the United
States. Prepared by Agriculture Canada
and the United States Department of
Agriculture (USDA) respectively, the
maps mark cooler areas with lower zone
numbers. To use the maps, find the zone
where you live and, in reading the pre-
ceding alphabetical list of ground covers,
take most notice of the recommendations
of botanists living in your own climatic
zone or in zones with lower numbers.
Plants found to be successful in those
zones should be successful for you,
whereas those that grow in zones with
higher numbers may not be winter hardy
in your area.

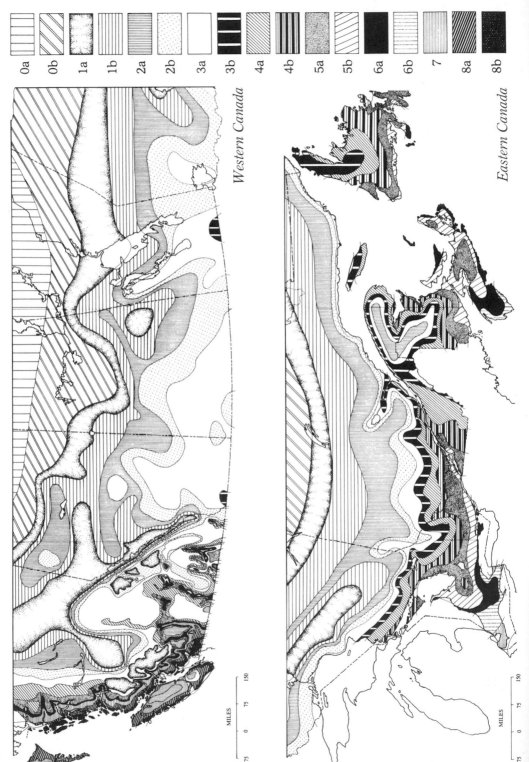

0a　0b　1a　1b　2a　2b　3a　3b　4a　4b　5a　5b　6a　6b　7　8a　8b

Western Canada

Eastern Canada

MILES
75　0　75　150

MILES
75　0　75　150

86

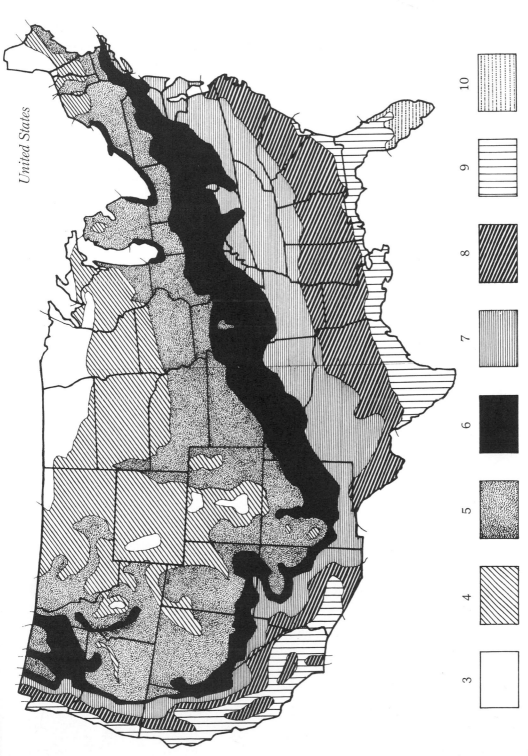

United States

3
4
5
6
7
8
9
10

Plants

While it is generally the best policy to buy plants from one's own country — delays caused by red tape and lengthy mailing distances lessen the chance of plant survival — some of the following companies will accept foreign orders. Canadians wishing to buy from U.S. nurseries should obtain an "application form for permit to import" from The Permit Office, Plant Health Division, Agriculture Canada, Ottawa, Ontario K1A 0C6. Request one application for each company from which you will order plants.

Canada

C.A. Cruickshank, Inc.
1015 Mount Pleasant Road
Toronto, Ontario M4P 2M1
Flowering bulbs, clematis, day lilies, hostas and woodland plants. Three catalogues (spring, midseason and fall) $3.

Gardenimport
Box 760
Thornhill, Ontario L3T 4A5
Flowering bulbs, irises, lilies, ferns and woodland plants. Catalogue $2 for 4 years (the catalogues are issued annually).

Hazelgrove Gardens
S11, C11, RR 5
Kelowna, British Columbia V1X 4K4
Perennial flowers and herbs to British Columbia, Alberta and Saskatchewan only. Send SAE for price list.
F.P. Healy
Box 6
Belmont, Manitoba R0K 0C0

Perennial plants. Catalogue $1
refundable.

Honeywood Lilies & Nursery
Box 63
Parkside, Saskatchewan S0J 2A0
Specialists in hardy lilies, but
Honeywood sells general nursery stock
as well. Lily catalogue $1.

Hopestead Gardens
6605 Hopedale Road
RR 4
Sardis, British Columbia V0X 1Y0
Hardy perennial flowers, including
some suitable for ground covering.
Price list free.

Hortico, Inc.
RR 1
Waterdown, Ontario L0R 2H0
An excellent selection of ornamental
grasses, ferns and ground covers. Price
list free.

V. Kraus Nurseries, Ltd.
Carlisle, Ontario L0R 1H0
General nursery stock listed without
descriptions. Price list free.

Sears McConnell Nurseries
RR 1
Port Burwell, Ontario N0J 1T0
General nursery stock in a full-colour
catalogue, also available from Sears
outlets. Catalogue free.

Stirling Perennials
RR 1
Morpeth, Ontario N0P 1X0
Hardy perennial flowers ranging from
alpines to ground covers.
Catalogue $1.

Vineland Nurseries
Box 98
Vineland Station, Ontario L0R 2E0
Dwarf and unusual evergreens,
heathers, bamboos etc. Price list $1.

Plants—United States·

Klehm Nursery
Route 5, Box 197
South Barrington, Illinois 60010
Day lilies, hostas and other plants.
Catalogue $2 (U.S.).

Logee's Greenhouses
55 North Street
Danielson, Connecticut 06239
Herbs, ferns, flowering perennials and
more. Catalogue $3 refundable.

Musser Forests
Box 340M
Indiana, Pennsylvania 15701-0340
Junipers, cotoneasters and a few other
ground covers. Catalogue free.

Red's Rhodies & Alpine Gardens
15920 S.W. Oberst Lane
Sherwood, Oregon 97140
Sempervivums and sedums, as well as
other plants. Price list 50 cents.

Washington Evergreen Nursery
Box 388
Brooks Branch Road
Leicester, North Carolina 28748
Specialists in dwarf conifers.
Catalogue $2 (U.S.).

Plants—Other Countries

Hillier Nurseries Ltd.
Ampfield House
Ampfield, Romsey
Hants S051 9PA, England
Twenty-six types of euonymus, 67
heathers and much more. Catalogue
50p.

Seeds

Abundant Life Seed Foundation
Box 772
Port Townsend, Washington 98368
Seeds of native plants of Pacific

Northwest. Catalogue $1 (U.S.).

Aimers Wildflower Seeds
Cotswolds, The Green Lane
RR 1
King City, Ontario L0G 1K0
Wildflower mixtures. Price list $1.

Bishop Seeds Ltd.
Box 338
Belleville, Ontario K8N 5A5
A good selection of wildflower
mixtures and lawn seeds. Catalogue
free to Canada only.

J.L. Hudson, Seedsman
Box 1058
Redwood City, California 94064
Seeds from around the world.
Catalogue $1 (U.S.).

International Seed Supplies
Box 538
Nowra, New South Wales
Australia 2541
Seeds of trees, shrubs, vines,
ground covers.
Catalogue $3 (Aus).

Maver Nursery — Rare Seeds
Route 2, Box 265B
Asheville, North Carolina 28805
Seeds for trees, shrubs, ground
covers, flowers.
Price list $1 (U.S.).

McLaughlin's
Buttercup's Acre
Box 550
Mead, Washington 99021-0550
Herbs, wildflowers.
Catalogue $1 (U.S.).

Mellinger's Inc.
2310 W. South Range Road
North Lima, Ohio 44452
Lawn grasses, wildflowers, other
seeds. Catalogue $2 (U.S.) to Canada;
free to U.S.

Park Seed Co., Inc.
Cokesbury Road
Greenwood, South Carolina
29647-0001
Seeds of flowers, ground covers.
Catalogue free.

Recor Tree Seed
640 El Paso Street
Denver, Colorado 80221
Seeds for trees. Price list free.

Redwood City Seed Co.
Box 361
Redwood City, California 94064
Seeds from around the world.
Catalogue $1 (U.S.).

Richters
Box 26
Goodwood, Ontario L0C 1A0
Herbs seeds. Catalogue $2.50.

Thompson and Morgan
Box 1308
Jackson, New Jersey 08527
Seeds for herbs, flowers and many
ground covers. Catalogue free.

Index

93

Credits